CRETE

archaeological sites, towns and villages

a guide to the island with 37 routes...
with history, art, folklore
with 169 colour photos, maps and plans

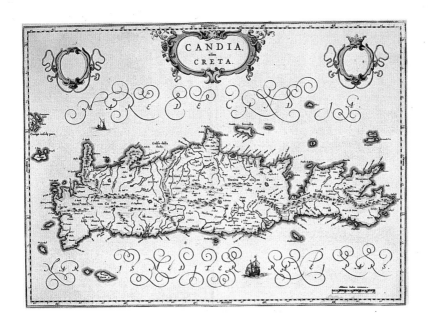

EDITIONS

TOUBI'S ®
ΕΚΔΟΣΕΙΣ

Texts: KIKI SANTORINAIOU
Trips - Maps: NORA DRAMITINOU-ANASTASOGLOU
Photographs: G. YIANNELOS, B. DROSOS, N. KONTOS, M. TOUMBIS

Artwork: NORA DRAMITINOU-ANASTASOGLOU
Four-colour editing: YANNIS KOLLAROS
Montage: VASILIS KOROVILAS
Printed by: M. TOUMBIS GRAPHIC ARTS SA, Athens - Tel. no. 9923874

mail toubis@compulink.gr

Weep not for the man of courage
Even if his shot is wide of the mark;
Even if he misses once and twice
He'll still be a man of courage!
And still his door will stand open...

("Rizitiko" song)

Foreword

Crete, the largest of the Greek islands, is a different world, one which floods its visitors with unforgettable memories. Its charm lies in the nature of its landscape and in its indissoluble bonds with its historical past: there is not an inch of land on this island which does not bear some trace of the presence of man since before the beginning of recorded history. There are prehistoric towns, the superbly delicate Minoan palaces, Roman ruins, Byzantine churches, Venetian castles and Turkish minarets, but also concrete pillboxes left over from the Second World War — constant reminders of how stormy life was in Crete in the past, and even in the present.

Almost untouched in many places by the wave of tourism that has broken across it, Crete is a wonderful encapsulation of the essence of a typically Greek phenomenon: a rich and historic past combined with an equally important present. Modern developments have not done much to deprive Crete of its ruggedness and simplicity — Crete, that beacon of European civilisation.

Yet Crete is far from consisting only of beautiful landscapes and antiquities. It is the people of the island who bring visitors back again and again. As you read this book, you will come to see some of the features of the island — only some, because the rest await you on Crete!

In Crete, hospitality is a way of life. The soul of Crete is not the creation only of its mountains, its sea, the blinding clarity of its light; above all, it is the creation of the people who live there, the proud Cretans!

Contents

MYTHOLOGY

The mythology of Crete is very rich. Whole volumes could be devoted to it, given that its prehistoric civilisation was closely bound up with the myths of the ancient Greeks about their gods and about the way the world was created: for this was the birthplace of Zeus. According to the tradition of the myths, Rhea, with the help of Uranus and Gaea, hid the new-born Zeus in the Idaean Cave to protect him from his father Kronos, who devoured his children in the fear that one of them would usurp his throne. Rhea then swaddled a long stone, which Kronos swallowed without realised it was not a baby. The divine infant was cared for by the Nymphs, while a goat, Amaltheia, suckled him on her milk. When the baby cried, the Kouretes danced the "pyrrichios" war-dance outside the cave, beating their spears upon their shields to keep the noise from the ears of Kronos. When Zeus grew up, he overcame his father and ruled the world, which he governed with the other eleven gods. Zeus' union with Europa, daughter of the king of Phoenicia, produced Minos, Radamanthys and Sarpedon.

Minos, who is both a mythical and historical figure, was the founder of Cretan sea-power, a wise law-giver and the head of the Minoan religion. The technological progress and development of Minoan civilisation as created by Minos is reflected in the myth of the visit to the island of the craftsman and inventor Daedalus. He it was who built the Labyrinth, the endless maze of passages and dead-ends, so easy to enter and so difficult to leave. Locked up in the Labyrinth was the Minotaur, a monster with the head of a bull and the body of a man, which lived on human blood.

As always with the myths, it is difficult to say where the truth ends and the story begins. Until the late 19th century, almost all our knowledge of ancient Crete was derived from the Greek myths. Yet as the ruins of the palace of Knossos were gradually unearthed, a real labyrinth of rooms came to light, most of them tiny and linked by a network of corridors. And the myth of the death of the Minotaur at the hands of Theseus suddenly came to life: it was easy to imagine the Athenian hero lost in the maze. Today, then, we know that there must be some truth in the Minotaur myth — the myth of the monster whom Minos kept shut up in his labyrinth beneath the palace and whom he fed on the tribute of young men and women sent by Athens each year as a kind of taxation. The myth indicates, too, the power of Minos and the subjugation of Athens to Crete — at least until Theseus killed the Minotaur and managed to escape from the labyrinth with the help of Ariadne.

More of the myth has been confirmed by archaeology: apart from the maze of rooms in the palace of Knossos, so reminiscent of the labyrinth of the myth, the double-axe symbol (the 'labrys') is constantly repeated as a motif in Minoan art, and bulls constitute a recurrent theme in Minoan palace wall-paintings.

Zeus, transformed into a bull, stealing Europa. Minos was produced of their union.

(wall-painting from Pompeii).

HISTORY

Crete lies in the centre of the eastern Mediterranean basin, one of the world's most important areas — an area where civilisations of great importance developed and where the fundamental ideas which even today influence most of mankind were born. The most important period in Cretan history was the Minoan period, which lasted some ten centuries. It was the nucleus for the creation of the first Greek state, of the first religion and of the first Greek art. The history of Crete began some 4,000 years ago. The island grew into an unrivalled thalassocracy with a brilliant culture whose most outstanding remnants are the magnificent palaces at Knossos, Phaestos, Mallia, Kato Zakro and elsewhere. The zenith of this millenium of history was reached between approximately 1700 and 1400 BC. But the fearsome catastrophe which overwhelmed Minoan civilisation around 1400 BC was the harbinger of its end: Knossos and other cities were abandoned. The disaster may have been caused by the eruption of the volcano on nearby Thera (Santorini), but it may also have been the result of an enemy invasion, possibly of the Myceneans. Nonetheless, Minoan civilisation lived on for quite a few centuries after the catastrophe, while refugees sought shelter in other parts of Greece and may have brought Minoan civilisation to the mainland of the country.

A map of Crete and the Aegean Islands, showing the

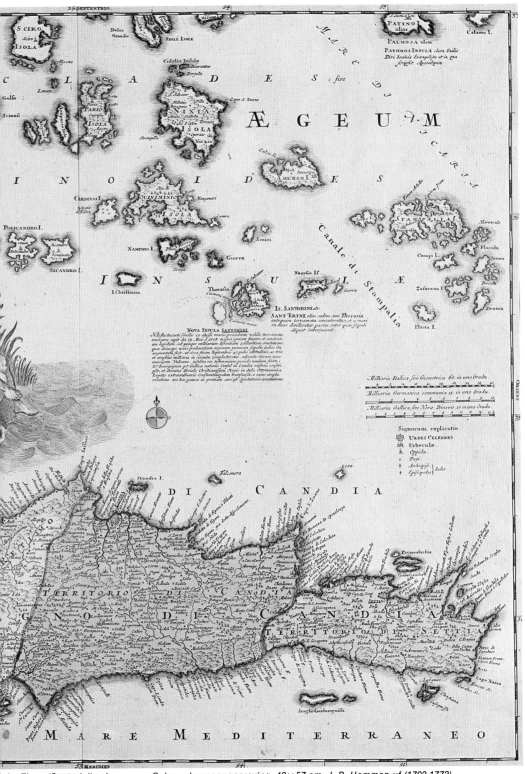

the Thera (Santorini) volcano.   Coloured copper engraving, 48 × 57 cm. J. B. Homman uf (1702-1773).

By 1200 BC Crete had been divided into a number of warring communities: its culture slowly declined and the island fell into obscurity. In the Classical and Hellenistic periods very little is heard of it, though we do know that around 100 BC it was a nest of pirates.

Between 69 BC and 330 AD Crete was part of the Roman Empire and Gortyn was its capital. When the Roman Empire split into its eastern and western parts, Crete joined the eastern (Byzantine) Empire and remained there from the 5th to the 9th centuries. In 824 it fell into the hands of the Arabs, who held it until 961, the year in which it was liberated by general Nicephorus Phocas, who returned it to Byzantium. In 1210, when the Crusaders overran the Byzantine Empire, Crete was given to the Venetians. Their occupation lasted until 1669, when Handak (Herakleio) fell to the Turks after a siege which lasted 21 whole years. The Turkish occupation of Crete lasted from 1669 to 1898. After a bitter struggle and the intervention of Greece's allied powers, Crete was granted autonomous status. Union with Greece eventually came about in 1913.

During the Second World War, Crete was captured by German troops landed by parachute despite the stiff resistance put up by the islanders: this fighting became known as the Battle of Crete. The resistance of the Cretan people continued throughout the occupation and led to many thousands of executions and the obliteration of whole villages.

The most important period in the history of Crete was the Minoan epoch. The superb palace of Knossos is the finest example of the architecture of this period. (In the photograph, the South Propylaea).

Prehistoric and Minoan periods

Gold pommel of a Cretan sword from Mallia, 1700 BC. (Herakleio Museum).

A Minoan clay wine vessel of the 15th century BC, found in Egypt.

The civilization of Crete is of remarkable interest since it was the first European land to reach any high achievement in art, architecture and engineering between 2200 B.C. and 1600 B.C. The chief cities of this pre-Hellenic culture were Troy in Asia Minor, Mycenae and Tiryns in the Peloponnese, Knossos and Phaistos in Crete itself. But as the chief excavations have been made in Crete, it is natural to regard this place as the principal centre from which civilization radiated.

The name Minoan has been given to phases of Bronze Age civilization in Crete. These are divided into Early Minoan 3600-2100 B.C., Middle Minoan 2100-1600 B.C. and Late Minoan 1600-1200 B.C. Each period was subdivided into three separate eras. The most flourishing period of this civilization was in the Late Minoan era and lasted for about a century (1500-1400 B.C.).

There is evidence that the Minoans traded with Egypt. Egyptian artists had an unfailing skill in depicting the racial characteristics of foreigners in the historical pictures with which they adorned temples, palaces and tombs. Among these foreigners we can easily identify the seafaring people known to history as the Minoans. At a very early stage they occupied some of the Aegean islands, making their headquarters in Crete. Eventually they dominated the seas, carried on an active commerce with all the Aegean coastlands and developed in Crete a very advanced culture of their own. Perhaps on the 13th or 14th century B.C. they planted outposts in the Peloponnese, at Tiryns and Mycenae. In Knossos, where their power was concentrated, they left the monuments of their engineering, architectural and artistic skills.

Though there is much Egyptian and Syrian influence, Cretan civilization always retained its European character. The dating of Cretan periods is founded on that of Egypt, by periods and dynasties, not by years. Thus Early Minoan was contemporary with the 1st Egyptian Dynasty, Middle Minoan with the VIIth Dynasty and Late Minoan with the XVIIIth Dynasty. This dating is established by the only method which, in the absence of astronomical information, can be considered accurate before the adoption of a fixed era, namely the finding of dated objects of one country with dated objects of the other country. Cretan pottery of the Early Minoan period has been found in Egypt with objects of the Ist Dynasty and Egyptian stone vases of the characteristic forms of the 1st Dynasty occur in Crete in the Early Minoan levels. The other two chronological contacts have been dated in the same way. The dating of the Cretan civilization is of the utmost importance for European archaeology, for though Egyptian influence was strong in Crete and in the Aegean, it did not go farther west, whereas Cretan

Bronze Cretan mariner from Tylissos, 1500 BC. (Ierapetra Museum).

A clay decorative item from Palaiokastro, 1500 BC. (Herakleio Museum).

The Cretan wild goat: a bronze statuette from Ayia Triada, 1500 BC (Herakleio Museum).

influence spread all over the Mediterranean lands.

The Minoan civilization lasted from the period when metal was first introduced, almost to the rise of the Iron Age. Even at the beginning of this era Crete had already had a long period of civilization, but she expanded rapidly and fell as rapidly. This was due to her geographical position, for being an island sea traffic was soon established with the other islands which were within easy reach, and for the same reason she was liable to attack on her coasts.

From the time that the island was first inhabited the Cretans were mariners, for all foreign products could only have reached them from overseas, and their own products are found not only in Egypt but westwards as far as Italy. They were potters even before they knew the use of metal, but their pottery, when compared with that of Egypt or Mesopotamia, is European in style and feeling. They were builders in stone at a time when the Egyptians were still living in reed or mud structures. They were weavers evidently, for great numbers of clay spindle whorls have survived—the looms, being probably made of wood, have perished. Oxen and sheep were domesticated, but there seems some doubt whether grain was known. In this the Cretans were more backward than the Egyptians.

It is, however, very noticeable that the great towns of Crete were built in close proximity to harbours, without regard to the agricultural value of the land, an indication that the maritime trade was of more importance to the Cretans than farming.

After trade connections had been established, Crete sent out colonies. Some of these were founded peacefully, some were due to conquest. The nearest land was the island group of the Cyclades, which had an original culture of their own, but which soon fell under the sway of their larger and stronger neighbour. Colonies were founded by degrees on the mainland of Greece, till the whole of southern Greece was so much under Cretan influence that it is possible that Minoan rulers reigned there.

In the Middle Minoan period the two great towns were Knossos on the north and Phaistos on the south, in both of which there were magnificent palaces. It is as yet uncertain whether they were the centres of two separate kingdoms or the capitals of one large kingdom. Until the Linear A script can be deciphered, our knowledge of the method of government and of the division of the island into kingdoms must remain incomplete. The later syllabic Linear B script, which was deciphered by the Englishman Michael Ventris, reveals that the language on the tablets found at Knossos was an early form of Greek. The tablets appear as lists and specifications of property, so many measures of corn, so many swords, so many

13

Clay storage jar in the palace style, from Knossos, 1400-1200 BC. (Herakleio Museum).

chariots, herds of cattle in the fields, as well as grain deliveries and imports of all descriptions. Clay tablets bearing inscriptions in ink have also been found. It is not known, however, whether the Minoans had a literature of their own. It would seem very likely in a civilization so fond of the arts and of the pleasures of life.

The brilliant, highly developed Minoan culture was brought to an abrupt end about 1400 B.C. by vast catastrophes accompanied by disastrous fires. Fortunately for Europe, the seed of the Minoan civilization had already taken root in the regions around the Greek mainland and the Aegean islands, eventually giving Greece its Golden Age — the achievements of which gave mankind its Western Civilization.

Archaic Period

After the collapse of the Minoan civilization and the destruction of the palaces, Crete fell into the hands of the Mycenaean invaders, the warlike Dorians, and "the island with the hundred cities" was divided into city-states which constantly warred among themselves. They united under Knossos only in the presence of a common enemy. Naturally, they could not maintain a civilization to equal Crete's Minoan past, but the creative talents of the older Minoan population survived for many generations and Crete flourished artistically to a remarkable extent. It was the period that saw the production of the decorated shields found in the Idaean Cave and the hammered statuettes from Dreros. The Daedalic school with its formal statues played a leading part in the beginnings of Greek sculpture. Fine jewellery and superb pottery were also produced at this time.

Towns like Knossos, Gortyn, Cydonia, Aptera, Ierapetra, Dreros, Phaistos, Lyttos, Eleutherna and many others acquired great power. But the strategic position of the island soon attracted the attention of the Romans who conquered it in 67 B.C. and kept it in their power for almost five centuries.

At Prinias, some 40 kilometres southwest of Herakleio, on a hill at the foot of Mt Psiloritis, have been unearthed the remains of one of the most important early Greek temples of the 7th century B.C. A great part of its architectural and sculptural ornament is housed in the Heraklion Museum. In the same museum are also the engraved tombstones which were used as building material in the construction of the 5th century fort on the hill of Prinias. The remains of another superb early Greek temple consecrated to Apollo have been unearthed at Dreros, a few kilometres from Neapolis. In the same area, farther south, on top of a hill which dominates the bay of Ayios Nikolaos, lie the ruins of Lato, an entire city with its Agora, Prytaneum, sacred and public buildings as well as a surroun-

A Cretan carrying a goat; bronze statuette.

A seated woman from Gortyn, 7th century BC. (Herakleio Museum).

ding wall. At Praisos, some 17 km from Sitia, there are ruins from all periods, but even in historical times it retained a very strong Minoan character since it was built in the 11th century B.C. by those who had been driven to the eastern part of the island by the Dorian invasion.

Gortyn, about 48 km south of Herakleio, on the road leading to Phaistos, was one of the most powerful cities. Among the remains we can distinguish traces from all periods from prehistoric times through the Byzantine to the Roman period, when Gortyn was the capital of Crete. The shrine of Pythian Apollo, the Nymphaium, the Odeon with its inlaid inscribed slabs which had been removed from the Archaic Tholos, the Temple of Asclepius and the Practorium, are some of the buildings whose remains can be seen on the archaeological site.

Classical, Hellenistic and Roman Periods

From the 5th century B.C. until Crete was conquered by the Romans the island was divided into small city-states. Most of them were surrounded by defence walls since there was constant fighting among them. The Dorians had by now established a predominance over most of the island, imposing their own traditions as well as political and social conditions. Their communities were ruled by high-born nobles who formed the city-council. This was a Dorian institution, like that of Sparta. The system of the city-state was fostered by geographical conditions. Each community held its own small territory with its central city and citadel, separated but not cut off from its neighbours by difficult but not impassable hills, which discouraged constant communication. This type of community developed into city-states each intensely jealous of its own independence. There were numerous such cities in ancient Greece. All of them had a bond of union in common traditions and reverence for the same gods, and in the face of danger from a common enemy they voluntarily united in battle. Such city-states in Crete were Aptera and Eleutherna, among others.

The Classical (500-323 B.C.) and Hellenistic (323-146 B.C.) periods contributed very little to cultural development in Crete. During the Roman occupation, however, living conditions were more peaceful and the population began to spread to the low-lying or coastal regions, forming large settlements. Gortyn became the capital of the Roman province of Crete and Roman buildings, monuments and luxurious villas were built in such places as Aptera, Gortyn, Knossos and Lyttos. The Roman city of Knossos was vast. It included an amphitheatre and a basilica, public buildings and the famous Villa Dionysus, the remains of which can still be seen, giving an excellent example of Roman architecture.

The upper part of a stone statue of a seated woman, from Eleutherna, 600 BC.

Medieval and Modern Periods

From the 5th to the 9th century Crete was annexed to the Eastern Empire, so called after Constantine the Great (A.D. 288-337) transferred the capital of the empire from Rome to Byzantium. In this first period of Byzantine rule Crete saw the building of its first fine churches with mosaics and pillars. St Titus in Gortyn is an example of this basilica type of church built by the Byzantines. Others are at Knossos, Chersonissos and Vizari in the valley of Amari.

After the Byzantines came the Saracen Arabs who remained in Crete for over 100 years (823-961 A.D.) There are no remains on the island from their occupation. Historical records tell us that Herakleio's market place during the Saracen occupation was a slave market where Cretan women were bought for the harems of the East. Although the Byzantines staged six campaigns against the Arabs in Crete, they were unable to recapture the island. In 826 the Byzantine General Carteros reached Crete with a vast army and fleet, but only managed to push back the Arabs and confine them within the walls of the town of Herakleio. A night attack by the Arab army took the Byzantines by surprise, almost annihilating them.

It was left to Nicephorus Phocas, a Byzantine general, to take Crete back from the Saracens in 961, after a four-month siege of Herakleio, or Chandax as the town was then known. Some 40,000 Arabs from Asia came to the rescue of the besieged Saracens, but they were ambushed and slaughtered almost to a man by the Byzantines. On 7 May 961 they charged into the fortified town, killing some 200,000 Arabs.

With Crete once again under Byzantine rule, the Christian religion was re-established. Herakleio became the seat of the Archbishop of Crete. Churches sprang up everywhere.

In 1204 Byzantium was overrun by the Crusaders and in 1210 Crete was sold by the Genoese Boniface of Montferrat to Venice. They remained in Crete for over 400 years (1210-1669 A.D.), with Herakleio (Chandax) their capital. They repaired the city's defensive walls, built a number of imposing structures: the Ducal Palace, St Mark's, the Latin Diocese, and the Loggia, a place of meeting which to the Venetians was what the Synagogue is to the Jews.

The Venetians were not oppressive rulers and the Cretans benefitted from their culture. Several Cretan scholars produced major works in those years.

During the closing period of Venetian rule, Cretan literature flowrished. One of the finest early 17th century works is the 'Erotokritos' of Vincenzo Kornaros. Apart from the world of letters, where the island produced great men of learning, the fine arts also flowrished. Icon painting also reached perfection, resulting in the fresco paintings of many Cretan churches, the work of such famous artists as Damaskinos, Klotzas, Theotokopoulos (El Greco), who later moved to Venice and Spain, and Kornaros who painted the great icon in the Monastery of Toplou.

In 1645 Crete was taken by the Turks but Herakleio held on under siege for 21 years (1648-1669). It was one of the most dramatic events in the history of the world. Finally, the city was handed over to the Turks on 27 September 1669.

During the siege the Turks lost some 117,000 men, while the Venetian death toll came to 30,000. The Venetian commander Francesco Morosini and the remainder of his army were allowed to leave Crete unharmed, after special negotiations with the Turks. Crete was once more plunged into poverty and cultural deprivation. In Herakleio the Turks set about giving the town an Eastern character and the Chandax of old never regained its former European aspect, though the old buildings were reconstructed and new ones were erected. Most of the Christians left the town, unable to withstand the daily ordeals the Turks inflicted on them. The period from 1770 to 1821 was the worst the Greeks of this island ever suffered — particularly in 1821 when the Greek uprising had already started on the mainland. This infuriated the Turks even more. In 1822 the High Commissioner of Crete, Michael Afendoulis, named the town Heraklion, after the ancient city of Heracleia, one of the seaports of Knossos.

After the 1821 uprising, an Egyptian viceroy, Mehmet Ali, was in command of the Turkish army in Crete. He recaptured most of the island by 1840. The merciless slaughter of Christians took place in Heraklion in 1898, when 17 English soldiers and the English Vice-Consul were slain with the Greeks. But the Cretan struggles for freedom came to a victorious end in that same year.

In 1898 the Great Powers, Britain, France and Russia, appointed Prince George of Greece to act as High Commissioner in the now independent Crete, a period that lasted from 1898 to 1913, when the island was finally united with the rest of Greece.

In our times the Cretans played an active and heroic part in the Battle of Crete (May 1941), not forgetting also the bold but costly act of rebellion during the Nazi occupation, when Cretan and British secret agents kidnapped the German commandant and whole communities were sacked in reprisal.

Crete Today

As a result of its position in the centre of the eastern Mediterranean basin, Crete has often been fought over and has been subjected to frequent efforts to dominate and control it. This interchange of conquerors, these wars and waves of destruction, and the constant struggle of the Cretan people for freedom have all helped to formulate the character of the island's people, their traditions and their way of life. *The five hundred thousand tough, proud Cretans who inhabit the island still live very simply in their mountain villages as well as in the plains with their orchards, orange groves and vineyards.*

Since the 9th century AD Crete has been obliged to welcome frequent invaders to its shores. Yet neither they nor the present-day visitors have been able to alter the character and customs of the island's people.

Nowadays the Cretans have discovered that tourism is a much more profitable occupation than their traditional means of earning a livelihood, and so they have set up the necessary infrastructure for tourism and hotel services so as to be able to cater for the many thousands of Greek and foreign visitors who come to Crete every year. Large modern hotel complexes have sprung up almost everywhere, and particularly along the north coast, where the largest towns are also situated. According to their taste and financial means, visitors can choose between luxury bungalows, small but comfortable hotels, boarding-houses, campsites and even youth hostels. *The bungalow complexes often stand on particularly attractive seaside sites where new hotels can often be seen in the process of construction. However, the atmosphere of the island has remained almost untouched, especially in the hinterland.* And although the weather in the winter months may not be so fine as in the summer, the island itself is a fitting recompense for foreign visitors who wish to get to know it during the cooler period.

As a place for holidays, Crete has a number of incomparable advantages. However, since its archaeological sites and other attractions are spread out over long distances across the island, visitors should always bear in mind that the question of transport often arises. The public transport system is adequate, providing easy access to most of the towns, villages and archaeological sites. The main road which runs from Chania to Ayios Nikolaos makes for fast travel along the north coast and enables visits to the villages and other sites near the shore or further inland.

Crete, of course, does not live solely in the past. Primarily an agricultural area, it produces cheeses of various kinds, wine, olive oil, citrus fruit and large quantities of fruit and vegetables throughout the year. Industrial development is limited. There are some small factories close to or inside the larger towns, and there is a constantly increasing number of craft industrial units manufacturing souvenirs, principally in silver, cloth and leather. Jewellery is made according to the ancient Minoan designs, and there are workshops turning out ceramics and icons as well as the curved Cretan knives famous throughout Greece.

Visitors who wish to explore the island in depth will never grow tired of it, but they should remember that in order to see Crete as it really it the main road must be left behind and the hinterland entered. *The hinterland of the island is full of surprises, often of the most unusual kind.*

When visiting the wonderful upland parts of Crete, visitors should bear in mind that the roads often come to an end in wooded areas, where the magnificent wild flowers of Greece, the vineyards and the orange groves often hide overgrown threshing floors, forgotten ruins and isolated chapels.

Sportsmen and women will find on Crete a full range of facilities for marine sports such as diving, water-skiing, boating and fishing. There are organised facilities near the beaches for tennis, mini-golf, volley-ball and basket-ball. The best period for hunting is from August to March (for pigeons and hares) and from August to January (for partridge and woodcock).

Agricultural Produce

The high mountains of Crete, with their snow-covered peaks, roll gently down to the sea on the northern side of the island, ending in verdant plains which are very fertile but small in terms of area. The southern shores of Crete are steeper, which is why the majority of the population is concentrated in the towns and villages of the north: Kastelli, Chania, Rethymno, Herakleio, Ayios Nikolaos and Siteia.

The south has only one large town, Ierapetra, and the smaller settlements of Chora Sfakion and Palaiochora. The fertile areas scattered across the island are used to grow more or less the same crops as were cultivated by its first inhabitants.

The large, fertile plain of Messara, watered by the Yeropotamos river, and the Lasithi plateau are the most highly-cultivated areas, while the Nida plateau on Mt Ida and the Omalos plateau in the White Mountains are much more barren.

The principal crops in the more low-lying area are citrus fruit (the island is famous for its oranges peaches, olives, grapes and carobs. There are also abundant crops of vegetables, fresh fruit and nuts. Thanks to its mild climate, the island is a major producer of early vegetables and particularly of tomatoes. The quality of this produce is very high and the quantities are sufficient not only to meet the island's own needs but also for export to other parts of Greece. In the higher areas, potatoes, onions and apples are grown.

Scenes from rural life:
The olive harvest;
Spreading out the currants;
Ploughing in the traditional manner.

Perhaps because of its climate, Crete has a seemingly endless variety of herbs and wild flowers. Almost all the species which grow in Greece are to be found there, together with 130 species which occur only on Crete. In spring, the air is full of the scents of thyme, sage and particularly of **dittany**, one of the native species. In antiquity it was believed to grow only on Mt Diktys and was held to be a remedy for complaints of the stomach, the digestive system and the spleen, rheumatism and arthritis. Hippocrates believed it was efficacious in childbirth, while Dioscurides described it as inducing miscarriages. Both Aristotle and Theophrastus tell of wild goats, when injured, eating dittany and then licking their wounds to heal them. Even today it is widely reputed to have therapeutic qualities and it is grown systematically for pharmaceutical use and as a beverage. Wild dittany grows in crevasses in the rocks at a high altitude, which makes collecting it rather difficult.

All the herbs which the ancients believed had medicinal uses can be found today in abundance, growing on the same hills and in the same ravines. The Cretans have only recently discovered the financial benefits which these plants could bring and have begun to market them in plastic sachets throughout Greece.

Dittany, known locally as 'erontas', an indigenous Cretan plant. Its light, fleshy, hairy leaves are turqiuose in colour. The purple flowers appear in mid-July. The plant has medicinal qualities and was dedicated to Diktyns or Artemis Britomartys, goddess of motherhood.

Cretan wine is justly famous. The red wines are particularly good, and so are all the wines of the Kissamos region. *Raki, the local spirit, is still made in the traditional manner.* If visitors are lucky, they may be on the island during *'Kazanemata'*, the days when the raki is made and the event is celebrated with riotous feasts. There is a tradition that Prince Henry of Portugal once imported vines from Crete to enhance the quality of his Madeira wines. Raki (or tsikoudia as it is known locally) is very strong and the islanders consume it in considerable quantities.

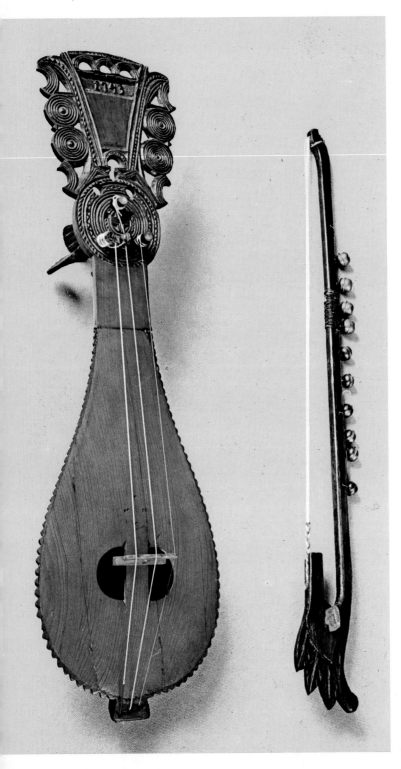

Cretan Folk Art

Since ancient times, the art of Crete could be said to be a direct reflection of the spirit of its people and of the singularity of its landscape.

The gentle contours of the mountains, the brilliant light which transmutes forms and masses into feather-light reliefs, the transparent sea and the azure sky, the legendary climate and the way of life of the people have all played decisive parts in shaping the intellectual and artistic development of Crete, since they have formed the natural background for all activities there.

Todays' Cretan craftsmen in the folk arts have the same sense for beauty as did their ancient forerunners, and using almost the same motifs they produce a vast range of folk art items all of which bear the stamp of a tradition handed down from father to son. This artistic activity, which has been preserved down the centuries, today finds expression in woven goods, embroideries, pottery, wood-carvings, metalwork and painting, to mention only the most important areas. Throughout the island, women will be found at the loom and men at the bench and the potter's wheel, turning out a seemingly endless variety of beautiful works of folk art.

The Cretans are past masters at making and playing the lyre!

The woven goods of Crete are designed with imagination and produced with the greatest care.

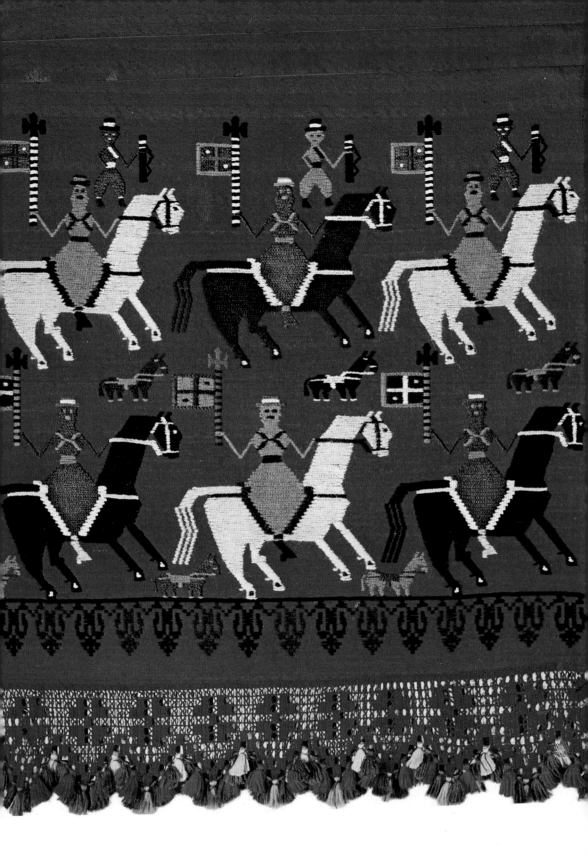

The manufacture and sale of these products gives work to a considerable number of people. Initially, of course, these items were intended for domestic use, but now objects such as **carved wooden chests, lyres**, etc. are much sought-after by collectors. There is also a tradition in the making of seal-stones, copies of ancient seals and carved stones. The gold and silver jewellery based on Minoan and Byzantine designs are of outstanding quality and there is a small industry which turns out delicate pottery decorated with motifs from Minoan mythology and history.

The Lasithi Folklore Museum.

Cretan woven goods are particularly noteworthy. The upright loom used in Homeric times can still be seen in many houses, as can the more **modern flat type**. Whole families are employed exclusively in the production of woven goods, covering all the stages from tending the sheep which give the wool to the process of weaving itself. Many of the weavers still dye their own cloth with natural substances, sealing the colour by dipping the cloth in the sea. Wool and cotton, and more rarely silk, are the most common materials. Cretan woven goods stand out for the wealth and vigour of their colours and for their designs, which are either geometrical or show animals and plants in the schematic forms encountered throughout Greek weaving.

Embroidery and lacework of unique beauty and the most delicate design have always been used by the women of Crete to adorn their dresses, their aprons and the walls of their houses. The vestments of the priests, too, were decorated in the same way. Even sheets, pillow-cases, curtains and borders were embroidered with work of the utmost detail, imagination in design and knowledge of colour. Sometimes the entire sheet or pillow-case was embroidered, and sometimes the needle-work was confined to the corners and edges.

The Local Costume

The Cretan costumes for men and women are very striking and constitute an important element in the island's folklore. Until about the beginning of the 20th century all the Cretans dressed in the local costume, wearing the formal costume on holidays and the simpler version on ordinary days. Today, of course, the costume is worn much less frequently, and will normally only be seen at official events or important moments in family and social life, with the exception of some of the mountain areas where the older inhabitants remain faithful to their traditional dress. The formal Cretan costumes, which vary only slightly from one part of the island to another, were in former times usually handed down from father to son and from mother to daughter.

The simpler version of the male costume consisted of the following components: on the head, a brack linen kerchief with tassels; across the shoulders, a cape with a hood to keep out the cold and rain, worn across the outer waistcoat and the shirt; inside the shirt, another waistcoat (usually short-sleeved and black); and round the waist a long belt which could be up to ten metres in length and inside which the knife was hidden. The final elements were the traditional baggy trousers, of dark-coloured linen, and the knee-length black leather boots.

The formal costume was more elaborate: the black kerchief with the tassels was silken, the outer waistcoat was decorated with special embroidery, the cape was also embroidered and the lining was silken in bright colours. The belt was silk and much broader, and the boots were white. As awhole, the costume emphasised the broad chests of the Cretans and their generally slim waists. The headgear is of a type found in quite a number of Minoan wall-paintings.

The female costume varied a little more from place to place. In the mountain areas, the form worn was called the 'Anoyeio costume', while that in use, in a number of versions, in the low-lying parts was called the 'soforia', which means 'town dress'.

The town dress consisted of a broad red skirt and a white silk blouse with loose sleeves, covered by the 'meidani', a form of jacket, or the 'saltamarka', a sort of bolero.

The Anoyeio costume differed from the town dress only in its lower parts, which consisted of long hemmed baggy trousers worn beneath the skirt and in the same colour as it. Two embroidered aprons, one smaller than the other, were worn over the skirt.

On their feet, the Cretan women wore black high-heeled pumps or white boots (stilvania'). A dark-coloured or white silk kerchief was worn on the head, and a gold crucifix, coins and other jewels were worn at the throat.

The traditional costumes of men and women are an important element in the island's folklore.

Local Feasts and Holidays

When the time comes to celebrate in Crete, they do it properly; the Cretans are not people to do things by halves. Wedding feasts can often go on for days. Among the essentials for a good wedding is the lyre-player with his three-stringed instrument and the singers of 'mantinadas'. Cretan dances are full of vigour and show and can be seen at any such feast. There are also countless religious feasts and local festivals where there will be dancing, song and lots of local colour.

These local holidays and festivals are also an opportunity to admire the Cretan costume, traditional folk music and the famous 'mantinadas', songs in couplets whose content is usually related to love but which can also be epigrammatic or tell of the pain of parting, of marriage, and so on. The mantinada is often sung by two voices, in a question-and-answer form. Among the Cretan dances are the 'pentozali', which is said to be a descendant of the 'pyrrichios' war dance performed by the ancient Kouretes, and the 'sousta', a dance of wonderful rhythm and superb technique danced in pairs.

Local feasts and holidays will also provide an opportunity to sample the strong local tsikoudia and gewuine Cretan specialities such as snails cooked in a variety of ways, artichokes in yoghourt, or pasta with smoked pork, together with the good wine which always flows freely and the traditional confections, such as 'kaltsounia', 'myzithropites', 'lychni', etc.

Most of the cultural and folklore events on the island take place in the spring and summer. At **Asi Gonia** on **23 April** there is a religious feast with a sheep-shearing cometition. On **27, 28 and 29 May** a three-day festival of folk dancing is held at **Chania** with Greek and foreign dance groups, in commemoration of the Battle of Crete. On **24 June** the villages of **Krousta** and **Piskokefalo** celebrate the ancient custom of the 'Klidonas'. The Wine Festival is held at **Rethymno** between **15-30 July** and there are displays of dancing as well as theatrical performances by Greek and foreign companies. The Sultanina Festival is held at **Siteia** on **25-30 July**. On **6 August** there is a religious feast at **Anoyeia** and at the same venue, on **15 August**, there is a Cretan Wedding, with local costumes, dancing and song. Another re-enactment of a traditional wedding can be seen at the village of **Kritsa** in the Prefecture of Lasithi on **26 August**. On **29 August** an important festival is held in the middle of the Lasithi plateau. The Chestnut Festival is held on **21 September** at **Kissamos** in the Chania region. **8 November** is the feast-day of the **Arkadi Monastery**, and the holocaust of the monastery is commemorated. **Herakleio** has a host of cultural events throughout the summer, focusing on the Kazantzakis Garden Theatre.

The customs and ceremonies surrounding weddings are still strictly kept in Crete today. The marriage procession, with its lyre-player, accompanies the groom to the bride's house, singing as they go traditional 'mantinadas' such as this one:

*"Open your iron-bound doors
And let us see our bride
in all her finery!"*

Geographical Description

Crete lies in the eastern Mediterranean basin and it is the Mediterranean's fifth-largest island (after Sicily, Sardinia, Cyprus and Corsica). Together with the islets off its shores, Crete has a total area of 8,335 square kilometres and according to the 1981 census its population was 502,165. It is surrounded by three continents, lying about 100 kilometres from Europe, 180 from Asia and 270 from Africa.

This position, together with the morphology of the terrain, guarantees Crete a Mediterranean climate which is among the mildest in Europe — in other words, it is cool during the summer months and and warm, particularly along the south coast, in the winter. The sky over Crete is rarely cloudy and there are long spells of sunshine. January is the coldest month of the year, and June and July the hottest. Even they, however, are much cooler than the rest of Greece thanks to the ceaseless sea breezes. The autumn, which often stretches on into mid-December, is perhaps the most attractive season, and it is, on average, warmer than the spring.

The island is set between the Cretan, Ionian and Libyan Seas. The water reaches great depths around its coasts, sometimes exceeding 3,000 metres. The coastline of Crete has a total length of 1,046.4 km, and consists of sandy beaches, picturesque coves and little harbours, and steep cliffs. The island is largely mountainous, and is crossed, from west to east, by the massifs of the White Mountains (2452 m), Mt Ida or Psiloritis (2456 m), Mt Dikti (2155 m) and the other, lower, mountains. In former times, the greater part of these mountains was covered with dense forest. Today, there are only two forests left: that of Rouva on the southern slopes of Mt Ida and that of Selekano on the southern slopes of Mt Dikti. At Vai, on the eastern extremity of Crete, is the unique forest of palm trees. As a result of the morphology of the terrain, Crete has a large variety of imposing ravines and attractive plateaus, not to mention numerous caves of historical and geological interest. The most famous, and the longest, of the gorges of Crete is the Samaria Gorge, followed by those of Imvros, Kotsyfou and Kourtalioti, among others. Of the caves, the most important are the Idaean and the Diktaean Caves, Skoteino, Eileithyia, Melidoni and that ot St John the Hermit. The most fertile and most attractive plateau is that ot Lasithi, and there are also picturesque plateus at Omalos, Askyfos, Nida and elsewhere.

At many points on the island there are springs which feed streams and rivers. Crete's only lake lies at Kourna in the Prefecture of Chania and covers a wonderful area of approximately 60 hectares.

The plains which are formed between the mountains are relatively fertile, and this is particularly true of those which lie along the southern coasts (the largest is that of Messara, which is 50 km. long and 7 km. broad). Cultivated ground makes up approximately 1/3 of the total area of the island, and the crops include fruit and vegetables, vines, olives and citrus fruit. Crete also has a superb variety of wild flowers and herbs, the best-known of which is dittany, a medicinal herb not found elsewhere. Another of

the island's unique features is its population of wild goats in the Samaria Gorge and on the islets of Thodorou, Dia and Ayii Pantes. Efforts are today being made to maintain the level of the population. Crete also has other wild animals and birds, including deer (which it is strictly forbidden to hunt), hare, partridges, wild doves, woodcock etc. Marine life on the beautiful sea-bed round the island is rich, too, with an abundance of many species of fish. Trout are farmed at a number of places on the island, including Zaro in the Prefecture of Herakleio.

It should be noted at this point that Crete can offer its visitors a very wide range of activities, including fishing, hunting and mountain-climbing. Because of the nature of the terrain and the short distances between high mountain peaks and sandy beaches, Crete is one of the few places where the incomparable combination of mountain skiing and water skiing can be enjoyed on the same day.

Administratively, Crete by itself makes up one of the ten regions into which Greece is divided. The island itself is divided into Prefectures, which in turn are sub-divided into Eparchies. The four Prefectures of Crete are as follows:

The Prefecture of Chania, whose capital is Chania and which is sub-divided into the Eparchies of Kydonia, Apokoronou, Kissamos, Selinos and Sfakia.

The Prefecture of Rethymno, whose capital is Rethymno and which is sub-divided into the Eparchies of Rethymno, Ayios Vasileios, Amari and Mylopotamos.

The Prefecture of Herakleio, whose capital is Herakleio and

which is sub-divided into the Eparchies of Temenos, Viannos, Kainourgio, Malevisi, Monofatsi, Pediada and Pyrgiotissa.

The Prefecture of Lasithi, whose capital is Ayios Nikolaos and which is sub-divided into the Eparchies of Mirabello, Ierapetra, Lasithi and Siteia.

The Greek Orthodox Church of Crete is autocephalous and is directly subject to the Patriarchate of Constantinople. The seat of the episcopal see is Herakleio, whence it was moved after the destruction of Gortyn.

Crete can be reached by air or by sea. Herakleio International Airport lies 3,5 km. from the city. Chania Airport is at Akrotiri, 15 km. from the city. There are frequent flights from the island to Athens and Thessaloniki. Siteia, too, has an airport, with flights to the Cyclades islands and to the Dodecanese via Rhodes. Rethymno has an Olympic Airways bus connection to Chania Airport, and Ayios Nikolaos to Herakleio.

There are frequent car ferry sailings from Piraeus to Chania (Suda Bay), Rethymno and Herakleio. Less frequent departures will also be found for the Cyclades, the Dodecanese, Monemvasia and Yitheio in the Peloponnese, Kythera and Antikythera.

As we begin our visit to the various parts of this great island, we should note that our purpose is to provide a guide to the most important spots which are of archaeological, historical and ecclesiastical interest as well as to the beaches of the greatest beauty and the best facilities. A fuller and more detailed description of the island can be found in our other publication, *Crete, Yesterday and Today*.

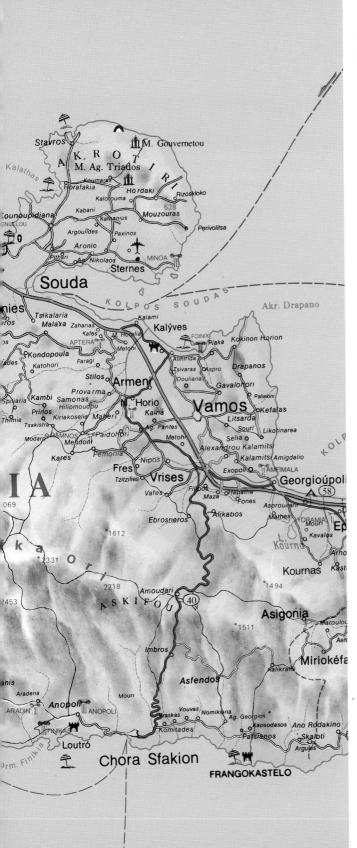

THE PREFECTURE OF CHANIA

The Prefecture of Chania occupies the westernmost section of the island and has an area of 2,375 km^2. Of this, 1,476 km^2 is mountainous country where wild hills are crossed by magnificent gorges (such as those of Samaria, Imvros, Therisos, Topolianos and Ay. Eirini). The vegetation is dense, consisting principally of holm oak, pines and chestnuts, and the sweet scent of the orange groves fills the air in spring. The steep mountain cliffs plunge down to superb beaches (Ay. Roumeli, Chrysoskalitissa, Sfakia). In the north of the Prefecture is the large plain of Chania, protected on three sides by the White Mountains. In the fertile soil of this plain grow most of the Prefecture's 17 million olive trees, oranges in groves like forests and considerable numbers of vines.

Large hotels have been and are being constructed all over the Prefecture and the infrastructure for tourism is far enough developed to meet the requirements of even the most demanding visitors.

By way of contrast to the archaeological interest of the other prefectures and particularly of Herakleio, Chania will compensate visitors more with its natural beauties and the magnificent variety of its landscapes. Nonetheless, there are archaeological sites, consisting mostly of Venetian and Byzantine monuments, and a number of historic villages.

Public transport within the Prefecture is served by the KTEL buses, while caiques ply between the villages of the south coast and sail out to the islet of Gavdos, the most southerly point in Europe. Chania airport, at Akrotiri (15 km from the city) has a shuttle service to Athens and daily flights to Thessaloniki. Suda Bay, Greece's largest natural harbour, is the departure point for the daily sailings to Piraeus. There are also less frequent sailings from Kastelli Kissamou to Monemvasia, Neapoli, and Yitheio in the Peloponnese, Ay. Pelagia and Kapsali on Kythera, Antikythera and elsewhere.

Chania

1. Lighthouse
2. Firkas - Maritime Museum
3. Nat. Tourist Organisation
4. Venetian Loggia
5. Archaeological Museum
6. Customs House
7. The Cathedral
8. Schiavo Bastion
9. The Naval Club
10. Buses to Akrotiri
11. Buses to Rethymno-Herakleio, Omalo, Sfakia, Kastelli, Palaiochora, Souyia
12. Municipal Market
13. Buses to Souda Port
14. Ionian Bank
15. National Bank
16. Bank of Greece

The city of Chania

The city of Chania is the capital of the Prefecture of the same name and is its commercial and administrative centre. It is the modern descendant of the ancient city of Cydonia, whose inhabitants were among the earliest populations of Crete. With a population of about 60,000, it is the island's second-largest city, after Herakleio. Chania captivates its visitors at first sight; it is a friendly, warm and unpretentious town. The Venetian buildings in the old town, now successfully restored, carry the visitor back to an age of greater elegance. And the large Inner Harbour, protected by its long Venetian breakwater and its fine lighthouse, brings to mind the period when Chania was a commercial port of great significance. Today this harbour is unable to serve the demands of trade; large ships cannot enter it because it is too shallow, and its role has been taken over by Suda, Greece's largest natural anchorage, which lies a few kilometres to the east of the town.

The old city is surrounded by verdant suburbs. One of these, Halepa, is worth a visit for its mansions and villas built in the late 19th century, when Chania was at the height of its power and prosperity as capital of autonomous Crete. The new town is well laid-out and consists of a number of suburbs which focus on the district known as Kastelli. This lies behind the bustling, noisy Venetian inner harbour and may well be the part of town which visitors find most interesting.

Chania has no large industrial units. Since 1974, it has been the home of some of the science departments of the University of Crete.

17. Post Office

18. Telecommunications Organisation (OTE)

19. Town Holl

20. Tourist Police

21. Stadium

22. Public Garden - Zoo

23. Olympic Airways Offices and Buses to Akrotiri Kydonias Airport

24. Historical Museum

25. The Law Courts

The city of Chania.

Archaeological investigations have revealed that there was a Minoan settlement on Kastelli hill, near the harbour. The city which later grew up on this site was called Cydonia and it was of considerable commercial importance in the eastern Mediterranean. Many ancient writers refer to Cydonia, but very little dating from the periods from Classical to Roman times has come to light. The town slowly declined, and under Byzantium was merely a little harbour from which a limited amount of agricultural produce was exported. The Arabs took it in the 9th century and gave it the name it bears today.

The first rulers to take any real interest in the place were the Venetians, who in 1252 began to build on Kastelli hill a town which they called 'La Canea'. The first defensive wall was built around 1300. During the 16th century this wall was extended and reinforced to protect the new quarters of the town which had sprung up. The harbour, too, was protected with a break-water. Work had been completed by 1590, but the harbour never became as important as the Venetians had hoped, partly because of its lack of depth and partly because of its exposure to the north wind.

Nor were the town's defences capable of keeping out the Turks; in 1645 Chania was the first Cretan city to fall into their hands, after a siege lasting 55 days. Chania was a Turkish city for two and a half centuries, until 1898, and in the 19th century in particular it was an almost entirely Muslim town as Turks from all over the island crowded inside its walls, seeking refuge from the constant revolts and risings in other parts of Crete.

After 1850 Chania was the political nerve-centre of Crete, and it never before or since prospered as it did in the period between 1898, when it was declared capital of autonomous Crete, and 1912, when the island was incorporated into the rest of Greece. Under the protection of the four Great Powers —Britain, France, Italy and Russia— the High Commissioner, Prince George, and the government of autonomous Crete had their seat at Chania. The mansions and luxury villas in the Halepa district remind us of those times; this is the quarter where the foreign embassies and consulates were, and the residences of Prince George himself and the

Chania.

politician Eleftherios Venizelos. Venizelos was born 5 km. from Chania, in the village of Mournies. He was the politician who worked for the union of Crete with the rest of Greece.

As the country's Prime Minister, he played a decisive role in political life and his political career was of great importance. Eleftherios Venizelos was one of the leading personalities in post-Independence Greece.

The **Old Town** of Chania is not very large (it has an area of about 700 × 700 metres), but its Venetian alleyways are unique in their atmosphere. Many of the houses which stood here in Venetian times have survived, together with a large part of the Venetian wall and the bastions of Sciavo and San Salvatore. Eleftheriou Venizelou Square, by the western harbour, has always been the centre of Chania. On the site occupied today by a new hotel was, in the late 19th and early 20th century, a club frequented by the naval officers of the Powers. Among the European ladies who made sure that these gentlemen were fittingly entertained was the famous Madame Hortense, immortalised by Nikos Kazantzakis in his novel *Zorba the Greek*. Today, thanks to its restored buildings, the Old Town attracts principally young people, to whom it offers an opportunity to enjoy themselves in a modern manner among traditional surroundings.

Among the sights of the old (Venetian) harbour are the long vaulted colonnades of the Venetian Arsenal, now used for exhibitions. Nine of the 23 areas in which ships were repaired and goods stored have survived. To the east, the harbour comes to an end at the Venetian fortress, which is worth a visit.

The Venetian side of Chania harbour.

The Venetian arsenal.

The **New Town** focuses on Kastelli hill. The total circumference of the outer Venetian wall was approximately 3000 metres, outside which there was a moat 50 metres wide and up to 10 metres deep at some points. Much of this wall has survived intact. The old Venetian town stood within an inner defensive wall of its own.

The *Municipal Market*, in the centre of the town and laid out according to a cruciform plan, is modelled on the market at Marseilles and was built on the site of an earlier market building. A wander around the market, with its vast range of goods, sights and smells, will remind us of the wealth of Cretan products.

The most famous church in the town is its Cathedral, dedicated to the Virgin, St Nicholas and the Three Hierarchs.

The church of St Franc,

The lighthouse on the break-water

The Municipal market in the centre of town.

which today is houses the Archaeological Museum, was the largest Venetian church in Chania. We do not know the exact date of its construction, but it was in place by 1595. A contemporaneous author wrote in a letter that during an earthquake which occurred in that year, "a crowd of people witnessed the belfry of the church fall on top of the church of Santa Chiara which stands exactly opposite it". Santa Chiara was a Franciscan convent and stood to the north of the Cathedral. It was built in the 15th century on the instructions of Pope Boniface IX. Nothing of it has survived.

The other districts making up the new town are *Ovriaki* (around the museum), the *Sintrivani*, in which Eleftheriou Venizelou Square stands, and, to the east, *Splantza* and *Topana*. The latter was the aristocratic part of town and had a large number of mansions as well as the consulates of the Great Powers before these were moved to Halepa.

From the old town we take the coastal avenue to the east, along the sea shore, and at the point where Akrotiri begins come to the pretty suburb of **Halepa**. This stands on a hill, and during the period of Crete's independence (1898-1912), the government buildings were here. Halepa was the site of the residence of Prince George, the High Commissioner of Crete, and the foreign ambassadors and consuls lived here, too. The neo-Classical house of Eleftherios Venizelos, standing in a square which bears his name and contains his statue, is interesting. The square also has a church of St Mary Magdalene, built in the Russian-Byzantine style in 1903 by the Grand Duchess Maria, sister of Prince George.

Another interesting feature of the town its *Municipal Garden*, laid out in about 1870 by Reuf Pasha to European plans of that period. It has various evergreen trees and plants and is one of the Chaniots' favourite spots for relaxation and contemplation. It also has a little zoo. To the south east of the Municipal Garden is the *Courthouse*, a fine neo-Classical building. To the west of the town are *Kotzabasi Square* and the *Rethymno Gate*. The *Town Hill* is of interest for its size and architectural style. This two-storeyed buildings occupies an entire city block and also houses the *Municipal Library*. *1866 Square* is adorned with busts of the leaders of the armed bands which fought for the freedom and independence of Crete.

The seafront at Chania.

The town of Chania has a number of interesting and important museums. The **Archaeological Museum** is housed in the restored Venetian church of St Francis. This is a splendid Gothic basilica with columns, which under the Turks served as a mosque.

The collection in the Museum consists of interesting finds from the Chania area and western Crete, including pottery, figurines, statues, old coins, inscriptions and weapons. Recent excavations at ancient Cydonia have further enhanced its collection with pottery from the Neolithic and Minoan periods, Late Mycenean pottery from Cyprus, imported into the area, and pottery with Linear B inscriptions. Also of interest are the Roman finds, including mosaics and statues.

The **Chania Historical Museum** is south of the Municipal Garderns and it includes one of Crete's most important historical archives. There are historic documents from the Byzantine, Venetian and Turkish periods, as well as more recent items. Some of the personal effects of Eleftherios Venizelos are also on display.

At the end of the sea-front, in the restored Firka Tower, is the **Maritime Museum**. The collection includes navigation instruments and historic documents, ship models and portraits dating back to 1821.

Crete, however, means above all sun and sea, and Chania certainly has plenty to offer in the way of beaches for bathing. Those who do not want to go far from the town will be pleased by the municipal beach, which has fine sand and lies to the west of the town. However, the sea is not terribly clean in and around the town itself, and the beaches to the east are not inviting.

To the west of Chania there are beaches which can easily be reached by public transport (in the direction of Kalamaki-Galatas). The more distant beaches (such as Platania, 10 km. from Chania, or Maleme, 12 km. away) can be reached by inter-city bus to Kastelli Kissamou. These leave every hour from the bus station.

A trip around the town before exploring the hinterland.

Trips from Chania

1. Mournies. 2. Theriso. 3. Cape Kydonia. 4. Kolimbari, Kastelli Kissamou, Falasarna. 5. Elos, Chrysoskalitissa, Elafonisos. 6. Palaiochora, Gavdos, Souyia. 7. Omalos, Samaria Gorge, Ayia Roumeli, Loutro, Chora Sfakion. 8. Vryses, Sfakia, Frangokastelo, Anopoli. 9. Souda, Yeorgioupoli, Kourna Lake.

With Chania as their starting-point, visitors can take shorter or longer trips to a whole host of interesting places: there are historic monasteries and archaeological sites to visit, gorges to walk —with the superb Samaria Gorge as the best of all— and fine beaches for bathing, with clear water.

1. Mournies

The pretty village of **Mournies** is only 4 km. from the city of Chania. It takes its name from the numerous mulberry trees which grow there. Mournies was the birthplace of Eleftherios Venizelos, and his house has survived. Today, it is a museum. Among other nearby sites is the *Koukounaras Mansion*, close to the village. This is a Venetian building with fine gardens and fountains presided over by a winged Lion of St Mark.

2. Theriso

The visit to the heroic village of Theriso is quite short (16 km) and very interesting. From the village it is possible to join a walking or climbing group for the ascent of Pachnes, the highest peak in the White Mountains at 2,452 metres.

We leave Chania in a westerly direction, towards Kissamos. At 1.3 km from the town we take the turning to the left (signposted).

The house in which Venizelos was born at Mournies. Today it is a Museum.

The road runs through the impressive Theriso gorge, 6 km in length and quite deep. Two kilometres before the end of the ravine, at the spot known as Gaidouromoui, is the **Kato Sarakina** or **Elliniko cave**. Finds from the Neolithic and Minoan periods testify to the use of the cave as a shrine.

We leave the gorge and enter a densely-vegetated plain, studded with cypress trees, across which we can see the village of Theriso. Standing as it does in a strong position on the foothills of the White Mountains, Theriso was able to take part in all the struggles of the Cretans for freedom. Under Turkish rule, the local inhabitants were in an almost constant state of revolt and some fierce battles took place. In 1866 the village was burned by Mustafa Nahayile Pasha, and many of the villagers, including the mother of future Prime Minister Elef-

therios Venizelos (the politician was then aged 2), were forced to take refuge in Kythera and the Peloponnese.

In more modern Cretan history, Theriso had its part to play. In 1905, Eleftherios Venizelos gathered his supporters there and proclaimed the outbreak of a revolution against the regime of Prince George, paving the way for union with Greece. Prince George was obliged to resign and make way for Zaimis.

In the village, one can see the 'Headquarters', that is, the house which was used by Venizelos. It is a picturesque two-storey building with potted flowers and an outdoor oven in the courtyard. High up on the right-hand corner of the house is the following inscription: "HEADQUARTERS OF ELEFTHERIOS VENIZELOS DURING THE THERISO REVOLT, 1905".

3. Akrotiri Kydonias

This is the headland which rises to the east of Chania and protects Souda Bay from the storms of the Aegean. In ancient times, the settlement of Minoa was located on its western side. In 824 the Arabs landed there. In more modern times, the area played an important part in Crete's fight for freedom.

Chania airport, one of the best in Greece, lies on Akrotiri at a distance of 15 km from the town.

A surfaced road climbs up out of Chania town to the east, with good views over the town, and after 6 km comes to **Profitis Ilias**. This is the historic hill where the revolutionaries of 1897 first massed, and here the Greek flag was first raised over Crete in February 1913. This is also the site of the **tombs of the Venizelos family**; there is a panoramic view over the town of Chania.

We continue, straight on, through a fertile landscape, and pass through the village of **Kounoupidiana**. Shortly after this, at **Chorafakia**, there is

junction. The turning to the right goes to Ayia Triada. We continue straight ahead for **Stavros**, which stands on a well-protected inlet on the northwest point of the headland. There is a good sandy beach.

Shortly after the junction at 9 km and left (15 km from Chania), stands the **Monastery of the Holy Trinity (Agia Triada) 'Tsangarolon'**. We see the imposing entrance to the monastery, finely sited, across a fertile plain of olive trees and vines. The monastery impresses both with its size and with its appearance and is in very good condition. It was built in 1612 by the monks Laurence and Jeremiah, who belonged to the Greek Orthodox Venetian family of the Tsangaroli, of Cretan descent, which gave its name to the monastery. It is said that the site on which the Tsangaroli brothers built their monastery was formerly occupied by a chapel to the Holy Apostles belonging to the Mourtari family, a name which crops up in the earliest documents referring to the monastery. The monastery church dates from 1634 and is cruciform with a dome. The in-

fluence of the Renaissance on its architecture is very clear. The facade is imposing, with Doric columns. There are two chapels, to Our Lady Zoodochos Pighi and to St John the Divine. The high and impressive bell-tower was built in 1864. During the War of Independence of 1821 the monastery was burned by the Turks, and it lay waste for many years before being restored by the local monks Callopis and Gregorius. There is a library, a collection of Byzantine icons attributed to the painter Skordilis, and a number of codices, one of which dates from the 9th century. The Holy Trinity Monastery has been used as a seminary since 1974.

The surfaced road ends here, but a very poor track continues to the north east. However, it is worth taking the trouble to drive along it, as it leads to a monument of great historical interest on a site which will fascinate nature-lovers: the **Gouverneto** or **Our Lady of the Angels Monastery** (19 km from Chania). The monastery stands at a height of 260 metres and is one of the oldest on Crete, possibly dating back to 1537. It is said to

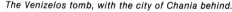

The Venizelos tomb, with the city of Chania behind.

have been built by monks from the Katholikon monastery, which was so close to the sea that it was forever at the mercy of pirates.

From the outside, the monastery resembles a fortress, with a strong Venetian influence. The church is rectangular, with a vaulted ceiling and turrets at each of the corners. The turrets have special slits through which guns and bows might be fired. The facade of the church is excellent, with fine Venetian carvings. There are a total of fifty cells, arranged on two floors. The monastery is dedicated to the Purification of the Virgin, or Our Lady of the Angels. There are also two chapels, to the Ten Saints and St John the Stranger. The Gouverneto monastery was destroyed by the Turks in 1821, but it was restored later and amalgamated with the Holy Trinity monastery.

The Katholikon monastery is nearby, at the bottom of a wild and magnificent ravine. As we walk down the path, we pass the little cave of Our Lady of the Bear. Inside is a chapel to Our Lady and an enormous black stalagmite in the shape of a bear.

We continue down the ravine, and after a further 10 minutes arrive at the Katholikon Monastery.

The white stone facade of the monastery can be seen from a distance, hewn from the rock above a broad and boisterous seasonal river, which is crossed, at its narrowest point, by a stone bridge 50 m. long and 30 m. high. Along the riverside can be seen the old sketes of the monks. A little further down is the famous cave of St John the Hermit. The cave is 150 m. in length and 40 m. in breadth, with a height which varies between 3 and 20 metres. It is very beautiful, with numerous stalactites and stalagmites. Access, however, is not easy. St John the Hermit, who died here, was one of the sages sent in the 10th century by the Byzantine Emperor Nicephorus Phocas to keep firm the religious sentiments of the people of Crete. Water trickles from the rock at one point inside the cave.

A further 20-30 minutes down the path past the monastery will bring us to an attractive deserted beach.

The Holy Trinity Monastery.

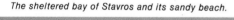
The sheltered bay of Stavros and its sandy beach.

4. Kolimbari, Kastelli Kissamou, Falasarna

We leave Chania in a westerly direction.

2.5 km Ayii Apostoli: A coastal village.

The surfaced coast road continues past the beaches of **Glaros, Kalamaki, Stalos** and **Ayia Marina**.

Off Ayia Marina, close at hand, is the little island of **Ayii Theodori** or **Thodorou**, which is a national park. Cretan wild goats are bred there and landing on the island is prohibited.

11 km Platanias: A tourist resort on a little hill, with a panoramic view. The sandy beach is 3 km long and 39 metres broad.

16 km Maleme: Maleme used to be the site of Chania's aerodrome, and it was the first spot to be subjected to attack during the German airborne invasion of 1941. The fierce fighting between Allied and German forces has gone down in history as the Battle of Crete.

After Maleme, we cross the River Tavronitis and enter the Eparchy of Kissamos. Kissamos occupies the northwestern corner of Crete. Thanks to its abundant supplies of water, it is densely vegetated, with numerous olive groves and fine chestnut woods. This verdant landscape, the interesting caves and, above all, its excellent beaches, have made the area of considerable importance for the tourist trade.

23 km: Kolimbari. The village stands among dense greenery at the head of the Gulf of Chania. It is a major wine-producing centre for Kissamos wine.

One kilometre to the north, on a fine site, stands the **Gonia Monastery**, a stavropegic foundation (one with special privileges granted by the Ecumenical Patriarchate of Constantinople). It has a domed main church with a narthex and chapels, surrounded by a spacious courtyard. Around the courtyard are the cells of the monks, the abbot's quarters, the refectory and storehouses. The Monastery is devoted to Our Lady Hodeghitria and has its feast on 15 August. The feast is also a popular celebration and attracts large crowds.

The Gonia Monastery has a important collection of late Byzantine icons, relics of the saints and other religious treasures. Numerous inscriptions are built into its walls. Today, it is the seat of the Orthodox Academy of Crete.

The road continues. Soon we have a view of the coastal plain, with its myriad olive trees, and the town of Kastelli Kissamou in the distance.

42 km Kastelli Kissamou: This is the most westerly bay on the north coast of Crete, lying between the Psatha and Gramvousa headlands. In antiquity, Kissamos was the most important maritime and commercial centre of western Crete. It was the port of ancient Polyrrhenia, but it was autonomous and minted its own coins, which depict Hermes on one side and a dolphin on the other. The city reached the height of its importance under the Romans, as can be seen from the ruins of its acropolis, its theatre, its aqueduct and the statues which have been found. In early Byzantine times the seat of the local bishop was moved to the village Episkopi. The town took its name (which means 'little castle') from its Venetian fortress.

After being destroyed a number of times, the fortress was eventually rebuilt from the foundations up by the Turks. It contained barracks, a church and a prison. Whatever is still

The beach of Platanias and the nearby islet of Thodorou.

A portable icon of St Nicholas (15th c.), from the Gonia Monastery of Kissamos, seat of the Orthodox Academy of Crete.

standing of the castle dates from this period.

Today, Kastelli is the chief town of the Eparchy of Kissamos and has a population of 2,800. It is a commercial centre, and the agricultural produce of the surrounding area is shipped out from its harbour. Wine and chestnuts are the most important products. There are ferry services from Kastelli to Yitheio in the Peloponnese, via the islands of Kythera and Antikythera.

We continue west from Kastelli, towards Falasarna. The road runs downhill and, 53 km from Chania, we arrive at **Platanos**, a modern village with extensive cultivation of fruit and vegetables.

56 km: Crossroads. We continue west (right), and after 5 km the road brings us to **Falasarna**. This is one of the best beaches in Crete, with clear greenish-blue water and a sandy shore. At the end of the beach, one can see the steep, rocky hill on which ancient Phalasarna stood. The surfaced road ends here, but a track continues to the ancient acropolis. Near the beginning of this road is a throne cut into the rock. Where the track ends, at the western extremity of Cape Gramvousa, we can see the remains of the ancient city, the most westerly in Crete. Phalasarna was built in historical times, was independent and autonomous and struck its own coins, which show a female head on one side and the letters 'PHA' on the other, framed by a trident. Phalasarna was another of the ports of ancient Polyrrhenia. Its harbour was enclosed, meaning that it was walled in and that entry was effected through a narrow channel. Today, the harbour

Kastelli Kissamou.

is 100 metres back from the coast and the channel is a cultivated field, for the level of the beach has risen. In ancient times, the safety of its harbour, the impregnability of its fortress and the fertility of its fields made Phalasarna an important commercial and maritime centre.

The city was entered from the sea side, and it was built on a number of levels, as can be seen from the surviving remnants of the walls, which were built using square untrimmed stones. There are also ruins of a temple of Artemis or Apollo, and even the foundations of houses can be seen.

We return to the village of Platanos. The surfaced road continues south, towards the coastal fishing-village of **Sfinari**.

Falasarna: the beach, with its blue-green waters, sandy strand and fertile fields behind.

5. Elos, Chrysoskali- tissa, Elafonisos

37 km Kaloudiana: A turning here to the left leads to Topolia. At 46 km from Chania, reach the pretty village of **Topolia** in its densely-wooded valley. The village has numerous springs and thick vegetation. There are quite a number of Byzantine monuments in the area.

The main road continues climb. At 50 km from Chania the road passes throgh the **Topolia Gorge** with its plane trees and wild olives. The wild and imposing ravine has walls which reach heights of 300 metres, with deep cavities in the rock. The road runs along the gorge and passes through a tunnel. The road through the gorge, 1500 m. long, is very beautiful and there is a particularly fine echo.

2 km to the south, is the cave of **St Sophia**, with a chapel, is to be found 80 metres above the road on a hill. This is one of the finest caves on Crete, with rows of tall stalagmites. The view is most impressive.

At 57 km from Chania, we come to the picturesque village of **Elos**, at an altitude of 560 metres, the highest on the route. After a further 5 km, a turning to the right leads to the village of **Strovles**, immersed in greenery and with abundant streams and plane trees, and on to Kandanos.

64 km from Chania, there is the village of **Vathi**. After Vathi the road becomes very poor, running south until, after a total of 73 km, it reaches the south coast at the **Chrysoskalitissa Convent**. The fortress-like convent is built high up on a steep cliff over a narrow bay, with a wonderful view south over the Libyan Sea. There are 90 steps up to the convent and, according to tradition, seven of them are gold, though sinners cannot see them. This is the origin of the name (which means Our Lady of the Golden Staircase). The convent was built under Venetian rule, on the site formerly occupied by a monastery of St Nicholas. Another possible origin of the name is that it comes from an icon of Our Lady preserved in the convent; the icon is more

than 1,000 years old and is gilded and carved. The double-aisled main church is dedicated to the Dormition of the Virgin and to the Holy Trinity. Its feast day is on 15 August. One kilometre from the convent there is a fine sandy beach, but access to it is quite difficult.

Continuing about 5 km south west from the convent, we come to the beautiful islet of **Elafonisi**, which is joined to the body of Crete by a shallow reef some 800 metres long. This is easy to cross when the weather is calm. The landscape is warm and welcoming, with brilliant white sand and the calm sea. There is no hint of the frightful waves which the south wind can whip up — some of the fiercest in the Mediterranean. Nor is there any reminder of the catastrophe of 24 April 1824, when, on Easter Sunday, the troops of Ibrahim slaughtered 40 Greek fighters and 600 women and children. Only a plaque on the summit of the island bears witness to their terrible end.

The Chrysoskalitissa Monastery, perched on top of steep rocks.

A shallow strait separates Elafonisi from the main island.

6. Palaiochora, Gavdos, Souyia

19 km Tavronitis: The village stands on the banks of the river of the same name.

26 km Voukolies: This is a large village at an altitude of 110 metres on the west bank of the Tavronitis. The road continues south, passing through **Kakopetro.** Continuing along the main road, we cross a fertile plain where the little River Kandanos flows all the year round. The plain is covered with olive trees and chestnuts. Naturally enough, the landscape is verdant and the area rich in the production of grain, wine and other produce. We now climb to the highest point on the route, the village of **Floria** at 580 metres. This village, with its panoramic view, is a cool and shady place to enjoy a cup of coffee or a glass of tsikoudia, the Cretan raki.

After Floria the road begins to run downhill, continuing in a southerly direction.

58 km Kandanos: This is the chief town of the Eparchy of Selinos, and it has a population of approximately 400. It stands on the site of ancient Cantanos, built in the 10th century BC after the Dorian invasion. In the Byzantine period, it was the seat of a bishop. The town has numerous interesting churches with wall-paintings dating from this period, such as those of St Kyriaki, the Archangel Michael, St Anne at Anisaraki, 2 km from the village, etc.

We leave Kandanos and continue south across a thickly-planted plain.

64 km Kakodiki: This is another village with a number of Byzantine churches, one of which has wall-paintings dating from 1387. There is a medicinal spring and the area produces large quantities of olive oil.

76 km Palaiochora: This is the southernmost town in the Prefecture of Chania, on the Libyan Sea. It has a population of 1,500, most of them former residents of Sfakia or Gavdos. The town straddles a peninsula on the southern end of which, in 1282, the Venetians built their Castelo Selino, which gave its name to the whole district. On the outside, the castle is quite well preserved.

Palaiochora has numerous churches and the ruins of buildings from both ancient and Roman times. On both sides of the peninsula there are excellent beaches, with fine sand and stands of tamarisks. The fine climate, the long spells of sunshine and the high temperature of the sea make this spot ideal for winter swimmers. The western beach, with fine sand and plenty of shady trees, is marginally better. It is 2 km long. There are more sandy coves to be found along the road to Yialos, at a distance of 7 km. The beach on the eastern side of the peninsula has no fresh water; there are pebbles and it is less busy. Still further to the east there are more little coves with sand and pebbles.

Two boat trips are possible from Palaiochora. The first is to the little islet of Gavdos, and the other to the coastal village of Souyia. In Palaiochora we can also decide whether to return by the road along which we came or to continue to Souyia and then turn north for Chania.

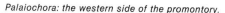

Palaiochora: the western side of the promontory.

The passage across to **Gavdos** is accomplished by caique. This islet is the most southerly inhabited extremity of Europe, lying 28 miles from Crete and approximately 150 from the shores of northern Africa. It is triangular in shape, with an area of 37 square kilometres. The 80 inhabitants are shared out between the four hamlets, Kastri (the 'capital'), Vatsiana, Ambelos and Karaves, a tiny harbour.

According to some, this is the mythial Ogygia, Calypso's island, where Homer says Odysseus was shipwrecked. As evidence, the supporters of this theory point to the cave at Errikia, on the north-east cape of the island, as the place where Calypso had her palace and kept Odysseus captive for seven whole years.

A beautiful bay with an excellent sandy beach (shade is supplied by scattered cedars and bushes) is only part of one's compensation for the voyage to Gavdos. The islet also has pine forests and a rare species of cypress grows there.

Souyia beach

Palaiochora: the eastern side of the promontory.

We return to Palaiochora. There are regular caique sailings from here to **Souyia** (70 km from Chania). The village stands on the site of ancient Syis, which was the port for ancient Elyros. No trace of this port has remained, however, as the level of the sea has risen. There are some remains of walls, tombs, altars and an aqueduct. An Early Christian basilica with coloured 6th century mosaics has also been discovered, and there are churches with 13th century wall-paintings.

Today, Souyia is a quiet, pretty village with an excellent sandy beach, 1.5 km in length, where the swimming is very good.

7. Omalos Plateau, Samaria Gorge, Ayia Roumeli, Loutro, Chora Sfakion

We leave Chania to the west, along the Kisamos road. After 1.5 km we turn left, on to the Alikianos-Omalos road.

The road continues through the lush landscape with its thousands of orange trees until we see **Fournes**, 15 km from Chania. Here the climb begins, as we snake up the side of the White Mountains. The route takes on a beauty of a different kind as the landscape changes entirely. Gone are the orange trees and their green and gold tranquillity; here the land is wild and imposing. At 24 km from Chania, we reach **Lakki**, a village of much historical importance for Crete. Thanks to its inaccessible position high up in the mountains, this settlement was able to play a leading part in all the island's struggles for independence and freedom.

We continue to the highest point on the route, 1,200 metres above sea level, which we reach 39 km out of Chania. Here we have a superb view of the Omalos plateau, ringed by mountains. The Omalos plateau, a legendary place of which many songs have been written, was for centuries the base of the fighters for the freedom of Crete, and many heroic pages in that struggle were written here.

When will the stars shine clear,
When will February come,
And I can take my musket,
Inheritance from my father,
And go down to Omalos,
To the Mousouri road,
And make mothers without sons,
Wives without husbands.

The Omalos plateau has a diameter of 4 km and three entrances: from Lakki, from Ayia

Irini and from Ayia Roumeli. The lowest point on the plateau (1,047 m) is in the north east corner, beside the road from Lakki. Also here is the **Tzanis Cave**, the deepest in all Greece at 280 metres.

The road runs across the plateau, and after a further 5 km ends at **Xyloskalo**, the highest point (1,227 metres) and the entrance to the **Samaria Gorge**.

Before entering the gorge, we should perhaps know that it is the longest in Europe, at a total length of 18 km, though the path through it is only 14 km long. The width varies from 150 metres to 3 metres at its narrowest point, Portes ('Gates'). It has been declared a national park in an attempt to preserve its rare flora and fauna. Thanks to the wild and precipitous terrain, this is the only place in Crete where the native wild goat (agrimi or krikri) still lives. There are also many rare species of birds and all along the gorge there is a vast variety of herbs (including *Origanum dictamnus*, wild dittany) and flowers. For that reason it is forbidden to hunt, to light fires, to pick flowers and herbs or even spend the night in the gorge. There are rangers all along the route and muleteers who, for a fee, are prepared to carry visitors for whom the walk has proved too much to the end of the route. Each visitor is issued with a ticket, free of charge, when entering the gorge. This must be returned at the bottom so that the safe passage of all the day's visitors can be

The first stop on the way to Samaria Gorge is the Omalos plateau, ringed by mountains.

Half-way down the Gorge is the village of Samaria, a place for weary walkers to stop and rest.

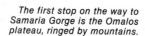

The Wooden Staircase and the chapel of St Nicholas.

checked. In the winter, the gorge is impassable, and entrance is only permitted from May to October. The walk takes between six and eight hours, depending on one's walking abilities. Visitors should have with them strong shoes or boots and something to eat (plus coffee if required). There is no need to carry water, as there are frequent streams of cool, clear water. The last boat from Ayia Roumeli, where the gorge ends, to Chora Sfakion leaves at 5 p.m.

At the top end of the gorge is the Xyloskalo, which took its name from the wooden staircase which once led down the side of the gorge. Today there is a narrow path with a wooden parapet to facilitate and protect those descending. As one goes down the path, the predominant feeling is one of awe; tall mountains tower to the right and left, while the gorge, seemingly endless, stretches out in front. There are countless shades of green to be seen, and in the distance another high mountain looms.

The descent is four kilometres in length, and the landscape alternates plunging depths with high trees, springs of running water, and enormous rocks which look as if they are about to block the path. After about 30 minutes there is a slight change in the view, as we pass the little chapel of St Nicholas, on our right, with tall cypresses, and two doors in the pronarthex. Now we are at the bottom of the gorge, and mountains whose peaks are close to 2,000 metres tower all around.

At this point the path becomes flatter. Every so often, smaller gorges run into the main one. The gorge begins to open out and quite suddenly the water disappears underground.

Here, half-way along the gorge, is the village of Samaria, uninhabited today because the wood-cutters and shepherds who used to live here were moved elsewhere when the area became a national park. The 14th century Byzantine church which survives has numerous icons and wall-paintings. It is dedicated to the Blessed ('Osia') Maria of Egypt, whose name was gradually corrupted to Sia Maria and thence to Samaria, giving the area its name. With its spring, the hamlet is an ideal place for lunch — and we are, after all, halfway along the gorge.

Now the landscape changes. The gorge narrows, and high rochy walls tower on either side. Shortly before the Gates, on the right, there is a little stream and a flat spot; ideal for a rest and a picnic. A little further along we come to the Iron Gates themselves; a truly magnificent spectacle. The walls of the gorge are only three metres apart, towering to 600 metres on each side. And through the narrow opening the blue sea can be glimpsed in the distance. Now the path runs along a dry streambed, on round stones. Gradually it widens out again and we come to another deserted village, Ayia Roumeli. One further kilometre over the same stones brought down by the torrent in winter will bring us to the modern village of **Ayia Roumeli**.

The Gates are the most imposing part of the Gorge. After passing through, the Libyan Sea can be seen in the distance.

The exit from the gorge is another of its pleasures. A swim in the Libyan Sea is the ideal epilogue to a long walk; there is an excellent beach with coarse sand, black pebbles and a clear blue sea.

Ayia Roumeli is a modern settlement, built on the ruins of the ancient city of Tarra. This was a small but independent city, which issued its own coins showing the head of a Cretan wild goat on one side and a bee on the other. It is said that Tarento in southern Italy (Taras in Greek) was colonised from here. A religious centre, Tarra had many temples to Apollo. It flourished during the Roman period, as witnessed by the numerous tombs and considerable amounts of jewellery found here. When the Romans discovered that the city had a temple to Britomartis, protector of flocks, they rededicated it to Romelia, their equivalent goddess, and when Christianity arrived it adopted the pagan goddess and turned her into St (Ayia) Roumeli.

Communications between Ayia Roumeli and the rest of Crete take the form of little boats. There are frequent sailings in the summer, either west to Souyia and Palaiochora or, more frequently, east to Sfakia.

The voyage to Sfakia is most impressive, with the mountains rising sheer out of the sea or forming little bays with tiny beaches, the haunt of nature-lovers. We pass one such idyllic spot shortly after leaving Ayia Roumeli, at the mouth of the little Aradaina gorge. In the next bay, at the neck of Cape Mouri, is the little village of **Loutro**, a pretty settlement on a tiny beach between steep cliffs. It stands on the site of the ancient city of Phoinica, and got its name from the baths (of which ruins can be seen) which supplied water to Anopolis (see below). A narrow strip of land on the seaward side and a small island protect the village from the worst of stormy weather.

Our boat trip continues beneath the steep mountainside as far as Sfakia or, as it is usually known today, **Chora Sfakion**.

The pretty village of Loutro can only be reached from the sea.

The verdant Askyfou plateau, surrounded by wild mountain peaks.

8. Vryses, Sfakia, Frangokastelo, Anopoli

We leave Chania by taking the old National Road to the north and west.

33 km Vryses. The village, a modern settlement, stands on the banks of the River Vrysanos, a shady place of plane trees and running water. To the east of the village on the road to Rethymno, there is a Greco-Roman bridge over the Vrysanos. Initially built in dry stone, mortar was added at a later date when the bridge had to be reconstructed.

As we continue, we see a green sea of wild olives, cypresses and ilexes stretching out in front of us. This is the **Krapi Valley**, the natural border between the Eparchies of Sfakia and Apokoronou. The landscape changes as the road becomes narrows, passing between steep hillsides crossed with huge oak trees. We now pass into another, shorter, gorge, the **Longos tou Katre**, 2 km in length. It is narrow and steep-sided, and its flanks are covered with ilexes and cypress trees. Here, in this gorge, the Sfakiots slaughtered 4000 Turks in 1821.

When we emerge from the gorge, we encounter the attractive and historic village of **Askyfou**. Because of its position, controlling the sole overland access route to Sfakia, Askyfou played an important part in Greek risings against the Turks. Today, it is known for its production of cheese, and all sorts of different varieties are on sale. The cafés sell cheese with honey, an ideal tit-bit to accompany a glass of tsikoudia.

Now we are on the fertile and verdant **Askyfou Plateau**, which is formed by the peaks of Kastro, Trypali and Angathes, and it is believed that it was once a lake. Even today water gathers there in the winter and slowly drains away to the north, at Chono. The fields are very fertile and potatoes, grapes and fruit are grown.

When we leave the plateau, we can see the pretty little village of **Imvros**, where the parallel route begins for the beautiful **Imbros Gorge**. When we cease to run parallel with the gorge, the small picturesque village of Imvros comes into view. **Imbros gorge** begins. The gorge is the route by which Chora Sfakion is linked with the **Askyfou Plateau**. The road is narrow, twisting and downhill. This ravine is narrow and deep, with a length of some 6-7 km. The sides are high and steep, and in some places come so close together that it is rather like passing through a tunnel. The trip is an enchanting one, with pines, cypress trees and ilexes on both sides and in the distance.

61

We come out of the gorge, after passing the turning for Komitades, and arrive in the famous village of Sfakia.

The village lies of our feet, nestling into the rock face. The houses, one above the other, are arranged amphitheatrically, with a superb view out over the Libyan Sea. Gavdos can be seen in the distance. The landscape is wild, harsh and grand, dominated by the White Mountains. The whole area is crisscrossed by gorges, ravines, difficult passes and wild mountain peaks. Even the beaches are hard to get to, and boats find it difficult to moor there. The name betrays this feature of the terrain; it comes from the word 'sphax', which means 'chasm in the earth' — the land of gorges, that is. Thanks to this position and to the bravery of its inhabitants, Sfakia was never conquered by the Turks and always played a leading role in the fight for Cretan independence.

The wildness of the terrain also caused the Sfakiots to turn their backs on the land and devote themselves to the sea. During Turkish rule, they were the only Cretans who carried out sea transport and trade — and piracy as well, an occupation in which even the Turks had to admire their prowess. The dense forests of the mountains which surrounded their home provided the wood from which their ships were made. The wealth the Sfakiots accumulated in this manner can be seen in their mansions, some of which are well into their fourth century of life. They are fine stone-built one or two-storey houses, with enclosed courtyards where the dominant element is the outdoor oven, and small door and window openings. All these houses were burned and looted in the aftermath of the Daskaloyannis revolt of 1770 and again in 1821,

on the outbreak of the war which eventually led to the independence of mainland Greece. The locals came back, one by one, and repaired the houses again, but Sfakia never regained its economic position or the full glory of its buildings.

The difficulty of life in the mountains and in this harsh landscape can be seen in the faces and bodies of the Sfakiots — and in their personalities as well. Authentic descendants of the Dorians, they are tall and fair-haired, with eagle eyes and lithe bodies which might have been carved from marble. The women of Sfakia, too, are among the island's most beautiful.

The Sfakiots are much attached to their primitive habits and customs. Even their speech retains many traces of its Doric origin. They are very superstitious, as perhaps is natural in a place whose landscape, with its caves and ravines, is easy to associate with demons and fairies. At the same time, however, they are very pious and extremely hospitable; it is a social obligation to treat strangers, and any refusal to accept will be taken as an insult.

A walk around the cobbled streets of Chora Sfakion will reveal the daily life of these people, unaltered down so many centuries. In the multi-coloured throngs of summer visitors, the traditional costumes of the Sfakiots and their proud deportment still stand out. They stand like ancient kouroi, bringing other memories to mind and making the thoughtful visitor wonder whether and for how long they will be able to resist the 'polish' of civilisation.

From Sfakia, there are two obvious excursions: to Frangokastelo and to Anopoli.

We drive east and, at the turning for Komitades, head right

and descend to the coast. **Frangokastelo** stands on a large bare plain. This Venetian fortress has survived in excellent condition. It is square in plan, with a tower at each corner. Over the gate is the lion of St Mark, emblem of Venice, between the Quirini and Dolphin coronets. On the seaward side of the castle is the ruined chapel of St Charalambos. The castle is associated in history with some of the fiercest battles fought by the people of Crete.

Near Frangokastelo is the very old church of St Nikitas. An annual festival was held here on the saint's day, with dancing and athletic competitions. Efforts are being made to revive it.

The mild, soft climate and the long and excellent beaches make this area ideal for holidays.

The road continues along the south coast to Rethymno.

We return to Sfakia and turn west and then north, where a passable road leads to **Anopolis**. This village stands on the site of an ancient city of the same name, on a small but fertile plateau, half-hidden among vines and dense greenery.

Ancient Anopolis was one of the 30 Cretan cities which signed the treaty with Eumenes II of Pergamum shortly before Roman occupation of Greece. It flourished in Byzantine times, as can be seen from the large number of churches which were built in Anopolis then, with fine wall-paintings. As part of the Eparchy of Sfakia, it shared the fate of Chora Sfakion during the period of Turkish rule.

Today, Anopolis is a pretty upland village with a healthy climate. The attractive Aradaina gorge lies between it and ancient Aradaina. A metal bridge was recently built over the ravine to join Anopolis and Aradaina.

The historic Venetian fortress of Frangokastello.

Chora Sfakion is built on the slopes of a hill and has a wonderful view out to the immensity of the Libyan Sea. The road to Anopolis can be seen winding up the hillside.

9. Souda, Yeorgioupoli, Lake Kourna

Souda harbour is linked directly to Chania along a 6 km highway shaded by birches. This huge natural harbour is the gateway to the sea not just for the Chania area but for western Crete as a whole. It is one of the largest and safest bays in the Mediterranean, which is why it is used today as a naval base. The small town was built during the 19th century as a base for Turkish soldiers and officers. The name is derived from the Latin *suda*, meaning a narrow passage. In the Middle Ages the bay was a lair of pirates.

At the entrance to the bay is a group of small islands, the largest of which is called Souda. In ancient times the islets were named Lefkes, and according to the myths this was the spot where the Sirens plunged into the sea and drowned themselves in their fury over being defeated by the Muses.

As we leave Souda on the way towards Rethymno, we can make a detour to visit ancient Aptera.

As we leave the main road, we come to the pretty village of **Malaxa** which stands at an altitude of 500 metres with a superb view of the plain of Chania and Souda Bay. Near the village is an imposing gorge with a length of 3.5 km and a depth of 400 m. The gorge contains some 100 caves. There are also ruins of Venetian buildings and Byzantine churches.

We then reach **Aptera**. The amazing view from the site more than compensates for the poor road by which it is reached. Aptera stands on top of a hill 200 metres high. At our feet are the blue waters of Souda Bay, with the Akrotiri headland blocking off the open sea in the distance. To the south, in the other direction, is the mountain scenery of the White Mountains, which for most of the year retain the snowcap which gave them their name.

Aptera was built in the 7th century BC and was one of the most important city-states in Crete. According to the myths, its name ('wingless') comes from the story of the Sirens, who in their rage over being defeated in a contest of music by the Muses tore out the feathers of their wings. Then, white and naked, they drifted down to drown in the sea, forming the Lefkes ('white') islands at the mouth of Souda Bay.

We return to the main road and enter the village of **Megala Chorafia**, where we bear left, along the road close to the coast.

18 km Kalyves: A coastal village with a marvellous beach stretching for 18 km. The village stands on a fertile site with abundant supplies of water and dense vegetation. The village is divided into two parts: the old settlement, with traditional stone-built houses, and the new quarter, with more modern structures. Nearby are the ruins of the Venetian fortress of Apicorno, which gave its name to the whole area: Apokoronos.

20 km Almyrida: A pebble beach with good, clean water.

30 km Vamos: Chief town of the Eparchy of Apokoronos, an administrative and commercial centre. The town takes its name from the Arabic 'vamos', meaning pass or crossing. Today, it is a quaint village with traditional houses, steeply-raked tree-lined streets and shady squares with enormous plane trees. There are numerous Byzantine churches, including one to the Dormition of St George. Every August, the local Cultural Association organises a kind of mini-festival.

39 km Yeorgioupoli. This is a coastal village on the Armyros plain. It used to be called Almyros or Armyroupoli, but was renamed in honour of Prince George, High Commissioner of Crete. The river Armyros, which rises in Lake Kournas, flows into the sea here. There is an enormous square with tall eucalyptus trees. The village has an exceptionally good beach, 9 km long with fine white sand, which is completely protected from the northwest winds that can make bathing on this coast hazardous. Thanks to its beach, Yeorgioupoli has recently developed into an important holiday resort.

It is possible to visit Lake Kourna from Yeorgioupoli. We cross the main road across a bridge and, after 6 km, a track leads to the lake and the village of the same name.

Lake Kourna, the only lake in Crete, covers a total area of some 15 acres. The circumference of the lake is 3.5 km, its surface area 1.2 square kilometres and its depth up to 25 metres. In antiquity it was called Cornesia and there was a sanctuary to Athena Cornesia. The current name comes from an Arabic word meaning 'lake'.

The landscape around the lake is wonderful. There is dense vegetation, with bushes, reeds and brambles. The south eastern bank is covered with olive trees. Beside the lake here there is a strip of white sand where a café serves tsikoudia and coffee and where a pedalo can be rented for a trip around the lake.

To the south of the lake, at Keratide, is the Kourna cave. This cave, discovered in 1961, has richly decorative stalactites and stalagmites and natural pillars. There are labyrinthine passages on a number of levels.

We can now climb to the village of Kourna. From the highest point of the road, the view of the lake is magical. The colour of the water can be seen changing from light green to dark blue, with the wild mountains all around reflected in the calm surface of the lake.

Kournas is built on the slopes of Mt Dafnomadara. It has many churches, including a 14th century church to St Irene.

We return to the main road and head towards Rethymno. To the left, soon before we reach the town, is the beach of Petre, which is the most popular area with the local people for swimming. There is an excellent view of Rethymno just before we enter the town.

Kourna Lake

The features which make Yeorgioupoli unique are its rivers with their clear water and the fine beaches.

THE PREFECTURE OF RETHYMNO

The Prefecture of Rethymno lies to the east of the Prefecture of Chania, between the White Mountains and Mt Psiloritis or Ida, which towers over the eastern side of the district and acts as the spinal cord of the island. Its highest peak is Timios Stavros (2,456 m). The Prefecture has an area of 1,496 square kilometres, of which only 596 square kilometres are suitable for agriculture; the remainder consists of high mountains and barren hillsides, for Rethymno is the most mountainous of the four prefectures of Crete. The population amounts to approximately 63,000, and their main occupation is stock-breeding, given that of the approximately 858,000 sheep and goats on Crete 193,000 are in the Prefecture of Rethymno.

Apart from the products of stock-breeding, the Prefecture also produces olive oil, olives, vegetables and carobs; in the case of the latter product, much consideration has recently been given to ways of making better use of them.

The Prefecture has excellent beaches and famous resort centres, such as Petres, Stavromenos and Bali. Along the southern coast, at Plakias, Ayia Galini and elswhere, are some of the best beaches in western Crete and comfortable resort centres are now coming into existence as new and modern tourist units spring up almost daily. Despite this, the Prefecture is in many ways one of the most traditional parts of the island, and increasing tourism has not encroached upon the agricultural and stock-breeding occupations of the inhabitants.

However, half of the beauty of Crete is in its mountains. As one climbs the sides of Mt Psiloritis, one's sense of the harshness of the upland scenery gradually dies away. Nature has endowed the rocks and the mountain peaks with such forms that, with a little imagination, one can see in them recumbent human figures, dancers or a human face.

The Prefecture is not famous for its archaeological sites, but it does have the famous Idaean Cave, where according to the myths Zeus was raised and where the spades of the archaeologists have brought to light offerings and Minoan finds. However, there is no shortage of sights, given that the Prefecture of Rethymno contains the heroic Arkadi Monastery, symbol of liberty, and the historic Preveli Monastery as well as a number of historic villages, including Anoyeia.

Communications between the Prefecture and the rest of Greece consist of a daily ferry sailing to Pireaus. There are also buses to Suda, where large car ferries serve the Chania-Piraeus line. From Chania airport at Akrotiri, Olympic Airways buses connect to Rethymno. In the summer, there are launch departures for Santorini. Inside the Prefecture, KTEL buses link the town with the villages and beaches.

In the summer, there is a caique service from Ayia Galini to Matala in the Prefecture of Herakleio.

Rethymno

1. Ligthouse
2. Venetian Harbour
3. Customs House
4. Fortress
5. Archaeological Museum
6. Arimondi Fountain
7. Tourist Police
8. Prefecture
9. Town Gate

10. 'Tessaron Martyron' Church
11. Ayia Varvara
12. The Cathedral
13. Neranje Minaret
14. Public beach
15. Iroon Square
16. Buses to Amari, Perama, Anoyia
17. Post Office

18. National Tourist Organisation
19. Town hall
20. Telecommunications Organisation (OTE)
21. Public Garden
22. Hospital
23. Bank of Greece
24. Olympic Airways Offices
25. Buses to Chania-Iraklio-Ayia Galini-Plakias-Arkadi

The Town of Rethymno

The town of Rethymno nestles against the edge of the sea. It lies approximately half-way between Herakleio and Chania, and for that reason the Venetian rulers of the eastern Mediterranean used it as a way-station and place of refuge.

Rethymno is the smallest of the three historic towns of Crete, with a population of only 16,000. It is the capital of the Prefecture of the same name, and a commercial and administrative centre for the surrounding area. This pretty and picturesque town has never been affected by earthquakes, and so its older quarters have survived in relatively good condition, with minarets and Turkish houses whose covered balconies —called 'kioskia'— provide an Oriental air to set off against the Renaissance features of the Venetian buildings. No other town in Crete has such a fine beach; the sand is fine and yellowish-grey and the beach itself stretches for a total of 16 kilometres.

The town has two harbours, one for largest craft and the other for fishing boats.

Since 1974, Rethymno has been the home of the Faculty of Arts of the University of Crete. In recent years, tourism has begun to increase steadily, and now there are hotels and other facilities for a considerable distance along the beach to the east of the town. Where there were once tiny villages, now there are densely-inhabited areas with hotels of all classes, restaurants and souvenir shops. The larger hotel and chalet complexes have facilities for water-skiing, tennis, surf-riding and other sea sports.

Rethymno stands on the site of an ancient city whose name, similar to that of the modern town, was Rithymna. It was first inhabited in Late Minoan times. In 1947, a tomb from this period came to light in the Mastabas district, but no systematic excavation of this graveyard or indeed of the city itself has ever been carried out.

The ancient city and its acropolis stood on the site now occupied by the attractive Venetian fortress. Ancient coins discovered from time to time indicate that the city had a temple to Apollo and a sanctuary to Artemis. It was never a leading political or economic power in antiquity. And later, during the Early Christian and Byzantine periods, references to it are few and scattered.

Rethymno: the attractive old harbour.

In the 13th century, the Venetians built their first wall around Rethymno. These fortifications stood to the west of the little harbour and were designed to protect the arsenals and residential areas. To the north and east, the line of defences lay along the coast; to the south, it lay parallel to what is today Palaiologou St and from the point where the Arimondi fountain was later built it followed what today is Mesolongiou St in a northerly direction.

In the early 16th century, the Venetians began to plan the construction of an out line of walls, in order to protect the town, which was expanding to the south. The plans were frequently changed, but in the end the walls were built between 1540 and 1570. A new wall parallel to modern Yerakari St was constructed, and the section of fortifications in what is today Martyron Square was reinforced with a bastion. A small part of this wall, the Great Gate or Porta Guora, has survived. To the west, near the seafront, was the Kallergis bastion with the St Athanasius Gate, and to the east the Santa Barbara bastion was built to strengthen the wall.

Directly afterwards, between 1571 and 1600, the Fortezza fortress was built on the hill overlooking the town. It is to this period, too, that the Loggia (c. 1600) and the Arimondi Fountain (1623), which stand in the centre of the Venetian town, can be dated. Three more churches were built; a Venetian chronicle of 1583 states that at that time Rethymno was inhabited by 213 Cretan and 84 Venetian families.

A typical alley in Rethymno. The impressive minaret of the Neranje Mosque rises in the background.

The attractive wooden balconies (sachnisia) steal a little space from the narrow streets in the old town.

Although the fortifications of Rethymno were built to designs by the famous military architect Sanmicheli, they were unable to resist the Turkish attacks for long. Thus in 1646, after a siege of 33 days, the town surrendered and was taken by the Turks. During the period of Turkish rule Rethymno was an administrative centre and its commercial harbour served western Crete.

During the Second World War, both Rethymno and its fortress were severely damaged. However, many buildings from Venetian and Turkish times have survived, and a walk through the old town will reveal genuine Venetian mansions and picturesque Turkish houses. The most interesting sights in Rethymno are as follows:

The Fortezza (Venetian fortress): The Venetian fortress dominates the town. Work on it began in the last quarter of the 16th century, and it was intended as a strong place in which the inhabitants of Rethymno could take refuge in time of need. Its walls are strengthened with three bastions on the southern side and one to the east. There were very few buildings inside the walls, and the powder magazines were placed on the northern side, which was better protected, in order to lessen the risk of explosions. Some of the buildings in the castle can still be visited: the water tanks, a Turkish mosque, a small Venetian church, the arsenal and the powder magazines. From high up on the walls there is a good panoramic view of the city and out to sea.

The Venetian Arimondi fountain.

71

The old Venetian harbour, with its vaulted buildings.

The church of St. Nicholas in the F

h was converted into a mosque.

Looking over the new town, from the Lighthouse.

A general view of the old town, with the beginning of its huge beach.

The Venetian Loggia: This was built around 1600 and was used as a meeting-place by the Venetian aristocracy. Here they did business, and here they consulted on political matters. The Turks converted the Loggia into a mosque. Today it houses the town's little archaeological museum.

The Arimondi Fountain: This fountain was built in the heart of the town in 1623, by the Venetian commissioner Alvire Arimondi. The vaulted roof was added later, by the Turks.

Venetian mansions: The building at 50 Arkadiou St must have been one of the most impressive Renaissance palaces on Greek soil. Only a small part of it has survived. At 154 Arkadiou St is the town's largest Venetian mansion, built during the closing years of Venetian rule in Crete. The large Venetian house at 30 Vernardou St is one of the best buildings in the old town. Interesting doorways in the Renaissance style can be seen in many of the alleys during a walk through the old town.

Santa Maria: The Venetian church of Santa Maria, of which two sides have survived in their original form, was converted into a mosque under the Turks. In 1890 a minaret was added to what was already the town's largest mosque. The minaret may be climbed. The Santa Maria church today houses the town's conservatoire and a concert hall.

San Francesco: The San Francesco church is a single-aisled basilica. It has a richly-decorated Renaissance doorway.

The Veli Pasha Mosque: Scholars believe that this large mosque, in the southern part of the town, stands on the remains of a Catholic church. It formed part of a Turkish seminary, of which 13 cells have survived. The Renaissance-style doorway to the mosque is of interest.

Rethymno also has an important **Archaeological Museum**, housed in the Venetian Fortezza. To the left, as we enter, are finds from the Stone Age which have come to light in various caves around Rethymno. In the glass cases on the right-hand side is a small collection of Egyptian works of art. Many of the finds, such as pieces of glasswork, stone seals and lanterns, date from the Hellenistic and Roman periods. An ancient shipwreck in Ayia Galini bay yielded many of the bronze finds, such as the statue of the naked warrior.

The Rethymno area is ideal for swimming. The organised municipal beach lies on the sea front and has fine sand and clear water. Rethymno beach, the longest in Crete, stretches east for 16 km.

Early evening at the old harbour: time for a last glance around before leaving.

The front of the church of the Arkadi Monastery.

Trips from Rethymno

1. Arkadi Monastery
2. Amari, Ayia Galini, Spili
3. Kourtaliotiko Gorge, Preveli Monastery, Plakias
4. Perama, Melidoni, Anoyeia, Idaean Cave
5. Panormos, Bali, Herakleio

1. Arkadi Monastery

Our acquaintance with the Prefecture of Rethymno begins with a visit, or rather a pilgrimage, to the Arkadi Monastery, symbol of Liberty and Self-sacrifice.

We take the Herakleio road. After 5 km there is a turning, which we take, for the village of **Adele**. The road runs through verdant scenery, and Adele itself stands among vineyards and olive groves. This was the birth place of C. Yamboudakis, who blew up the Arkadi Monastery. His house can be seen in the village, and his bust stands in the village square.

The road continues through the villages of **Loutra** and **Kyrianna**, both smothered in greenery, the latter of which has a 14th century church dedicated to the Dormition of the Virgin and St Paraskevi.

We begin to climb, and after 18 km from Rethymno come to the village of **Amnato**, which has an excellent view. To the west towers Mt Vrysakas, to the north east an enormous forest of olives stretches all the way to the sea and to the south we can see the height on which the Arkadi Monastery stands.

This village has been inhabited since Venetian times, as can be seen from the Venetian houses and the inscriptions on the gates. In the revolt of 1866 many of the villagers were among those who barricaded themselves in the Arkadi Monastery, including the heroine Charikleia Daskalaki and her two sons. Her bust stands in the square.

From Amnato, a narrow winding road climbs up through a green gorge with dense olive groves to the Arkadi Monastery (5 km).

The historic **Arkadi Monastery** stands on a fine site amid dense greenery, with an excellent view down the thickly-wooded gorge and out to the azure sea.

The date of its foundation is not known with exactness. According to one source, it was founded in the late Byzantine period (10th-13th centuries) by a monk named Arcadius, or alternatively it may be as late as the 16th century date on the belfry. It consists of a fortified building with two main entrances, a guesthouse, a refectory, a gunpowder store and cellars. The main entrance was destroyed in the fighting of 1866 and was rebuilt in its original form only four years later. Opposite the entrance was a windmill, which in 1910 was converted into an ossuary. The church was completed in 1587. The fine facade of the church, in a Renaissance style, dominates the whole complex of buildings, with their vaulted cells and Gothic windows. The church itself is a double-aisled basilica and it is dedicated to St Constantine and to the Transfiguration. Under the Venetians, the monastery was a very wealthy foundation, with 300 monks according to the traveller R. Pococke. In the 18th century it was known for its embroidery in gold thread and there was a workshop which turned out embroidered vestments.

The inaccessibility of the monastery and its castle-like structure, with high, thick walls, were to be of decisive importance in its history. In May 1866, when the great Cretan Revolt broke out, some 1,500 captains and leaders of armed bands gathered at the monastery to organise the rebellion and plot its course. The Turkish pasha at Rethymno immediately sent out a force of men to nip the revolution in the bud. By the time they arrived, however, the revolutionaries had left, and the

The Resurrection; a section of the burned screen in the Monastery.

"The flame lit here in the crypt,
4which cast its light over the whole of famous Crete,
was the flame of God, and in it
the Cretans were consumed in the cause of Liberty!".

The words inscribed on the marble plaque to the right of the powder magazine.

soldiers had to content themselves with wrecking the interior of the church.

After the Turks had left, the local people and the rebels barricaded themselves into the monastery in the fear that they might return. Although the monastery itself was not ideal as a place of safety, the abbot and the freedom fighters decided to use it as their base because of its advantageous position. In the past, the monastery had already been used for a similar purpose. So on 7 November 1866, a force of 15,000 Turkish soldiers with 30 guns set out from Rethymno and managed, passing through the gorge by night, to encircle the monastery by morning.

The unequal struggle thus began on the morning of 8 November. Inside the monastery there were only 259 armed men, together with 705 women and childern who had taken refuge there. Throughout the first day, the Cretans were able to beat off the Turkish attacks, but their position was hopeless. As soon as the sun set, Abbot Gabriel sent out two men to get help. Aided by the darkness, they managed to slip through the Turkish lines, but help was impossible to find.

In the meantime, the Turks had manoeuvred their two largest guns into firing positions. As soon as it was light enough, they opened fire and had soon broken down the main gate. The Turkish troops poured into the courtyard. Seeing this, Abbot Gabriel gathered all the women and children in the powder magazine, and they decided to blow themselves up rather than surrender. No one was willing to fall into the hands of the Turks.

The Cretans had fought so bravely that it was many hours before the Turks were able, despite their numerical superiority, to gain entry to the monastery buildings through the 8 metre wide door. Constan-

The ancient cypress tree on the northern side of the courtyard. The entrance to the guesthouse can be seen, together with the gate leading to the Refectory yard.

tis Yamboudakis was waiting for them in the powder magazine, pistol in hand. Wishing to take as many as he could with him, he waited until they had captured the door. The last act in the tragedy of Arkadi had begun.

The aftermath was tragic; 114 people were taken prisoner by the Turks, while three or perhaps four, with Adam Papadakis amongst them, managed to escape. The rest were killed in battle, slaughtered in cold blood or blown up. The Turks, too, suffered heavy losses: some 1,500 dead and wounded.

Arkadi was suppressed but not beaten. The marks of the bullets can still be seen on the trunks of its aged cypresses.

The pasha in Rethymno thought that his campaign had put an end to the revolt and that he had taught the Cretans a lesson by punishing the revolutionaries. But the news of the tragedy at the Arkadi Monastery spread quickly throughout Europe and produced a result quite unlike what he had hoped. The Great Powers awoke and began to look more carefully at the Cretan question. Thus the struggles of the Cretan people for freedom led eventually to the autonomy of the island in 1898.

On 7-9 November each year, celebrations take place in Rethymno and at the Monastery in commemoration of the self-sacrifice of the defenders.

2. Amari, Ayia Galini, Spili

We leave Rethymno along the road to Herakleio. After 3.2 km, in the suburb of **Misirgia**, we turn right. The road twists and turns up the hill, with superb views over the surrounding landscape, and after 11 km brings us to the village of **Prases**. This pretty village, with its many Venetian houses, stands on the slopes of a densely-wooded gorge. The church in its cemetery, dedicated to Our Lady 'Myrtidiotissa', has wall-paintings dating from the 14th century. The icon of Our Lady is believed to be miraculous.

From the exit to the village the Amari valley can be seen. From the same spot, there is an excellent view, behind and to the left, of the wild **Prasano gorge**. *Now the road descends, crossing a narrow old stone bridge*. We continue through **Potami**. The surrounding area is fertile and quite heavily cultivated.

The surfaced road runs on to Apostoli, 30 km from Rethymno. Built in the Byzantine period, this village stands at an altitude of 500 metres at the point where the waters of the Stavromana and Amarianos rivers divide. In the year 249, the Ten Saints were arrested here, and since then the village has borne the name Apostoli ('apostles'). It has numerous churches, notably that of St Nicholas, with 14th century wall-paintings, and that of St Spyridon.

The road continues to **Ayia Fotini**, where there is an important crossroads. The main road continues straight ahead for the Asomaton Monastery. The turning to the right leads to the villages of the Smylianos plain, and that to the left will take us to the picturesque villages of Thronos and Kaloyerou. If we take the right turning, the following villages can be visited: **Meronas**, with an excellent view and churches with 14th and 15th century wall-paintings; **Yerakari**, standing at an altitude of 680 metres on the foothills of Mt Kedros, a centre of agricultural production famed for its cherries; **Smyles**, a small farming community which has given its name to the whole area; **Vryses**, a densely-vegetated village with numerous streams and wonderful gardens; **Ano Meros**, another thickly-wooded village with the old Kaloeidena Monastery, of which the Asomaton Monastery was once a dependency.

The road to the left at Ayia Fotini leads, after 1 km, to the village of **Thronos**. Thronos stands on a hill called the Throniani Kefala, and has a wonderful view across towards Mt Ida, while the green Amari valley lies spread out beneath it. This was the site of ancient Syvritos, some remains of which have survived. Syvritos was built on a number of different levels; it was an independent city and reached the height of its prosperity and influence in Roman times. It issued its own silver coins, which depicted Hermes. Its outlet to the sea was called Soulia, a town which has been identified with modern Ayia Galini. In the early Byzantine period, it was the seat of a bishop, whose throne ('thronos' in Greek) gave its name to the village. It was razed by the Saracens, but the name of Syvritos continued to be used in the castelans, the administrative divisions into which the Venetians separated Crete.

The village has a Byzantine church of Our Lady of Thronos, dating from the 14th century, with rich wall-paintings and decoration. The church probably stands on the foundations of the cathedral erected when Syvritos was a bishopric.

We continue through the pretty village of **Kalogerou**. The church of St John, in the countryside near the village, has wonderful wall-paintings.

The road continues after Kalogerou, bending back to merge with the main road to the Asomaton Monastery.

35 km Asomaton Monastery: The monastery stands in a beautiful position, with a fine view over the highly-cultivated valley with its olives, vineyards, fruit trees, enormous plane trees and ancient oak trees. In the centre of its courtyard is a fountain, from which crystal-clear water flows in abundance.

The village of Thronos and Kaloyerou in the Amari Valley, with Mt Psiloritis in the background.

The monastery was founded in the 9th or 10th century and it is dedicated to the Archangels Gabriel and Michael. It was destroyed by the Arabs, but rebuilt in 1682 by the monk Macarius. The Turks burned it in 1821, but spared the main church. During the period of Turkish rule, the monastery played an important role in scholarship and education. In 1833, the abbot Joseph, who is thought of as the founder of the monastery in modern times, set up at Monastiraki a secondary school, the Hellenic Academy, the only place in the Eparchy of Amari where higher education of any form could be acquired.

Since 1927, the Asomaton Monastery has operated without interruption as an Agricultural School, with particular emphasis on stockbreeding. Its main church preserves icons of the Holy Trinity (dating from 1619) and of the Archangels, the latter being the work of the abbot Manassis and dating from 1755. It has a library of theological works.

Near the monastery is the interesting Byzantine church of **St Paraskevi**. A cruciform church with a dome, it was restored in 1888.

From the Asomaton Monastery, a turning to the right leads to **Monastiraki**. The name ('little monastery') comes from a church which had cells around its courtyard, like a monastery, and which was an offshoot of the Asomaton Monastery. This was the site of the Hellenic Academy founded by abbot Joseph.

Another road leading off to the right from the Asomaton Monastery goes, in 5 km, to **Amari**. This little mountain village (altitude 460 m) is the chief settlement in the Eparchy of the same name. It was first settled during the later Byzantine period.

We return to the main road at the Asomaton Monastery.

41 km Vizari: This was the feudal estate of the Vlastos family and flourished during Venetian times. The village contains the ruins of a mansion whose frontage boasts a sundial with Latin numerals. The villagers of Vizari founded Fourfouras.

44 km Fourfouras: This pretty and well-vegetated village stands on the top of a cliff (altitude 460 m) among the foothills of Mt Ida. It looks like

a fortified village. The most interesting church in the vicinity is that of Our Lady 'Kardiotissa', dating from the Byzantine period. At one time it was a nunnery, and it has excellent 14th-15th century wall-paintings.

After some bends and having crossed a verdant plain, the road reaches **Kouroutes**, at an altitude of 510 m. According to the myths, it was here, at the foot of Mt Ida, that the Kouretes (young warriors) brought up Zeus. In the summer, groups of walkers start from here for the ascent of the highest peak (Timios Stavros) of Mt Ida, at 2,456 m.

A little further down, at an altitude of 500 metres, is the village of **Nithavris**. We continue straight ahead and, at 55 km come to **Apodoulou**, at a height of 450 m. The village is quaint, with fountains and pretty gardens.

The road straight on (south) through Apodoulou soon comes to a crossroads for Ayia Galini. The road to the left crosses the Messara plain on its way to Herakleio (there is a bus service once a day along this route).

The turning to the right twists steeply down towards **Ayia Galini**, which it reaches after 6 km of wonderful views out across the Libyan Sea.

The pretty harbour of Ayia Galini stands on the sheltered bay of Messara, on the Libyan Sea under Mt Psiloritis. Its attractive beach, 1 km long, has pebbles of various sizes and, thanks to the mildness of the climate, the temperature of the sea is 18 degrees Centigrade summer and winter. This is what has made Ayia Galini such a popular holiday resort. Along the coast to the west there are hidden caves, accessible only by boat, with wonderful light effects as the sun plays on the water inside. One of the caves is called the **Cave of Daedalus**, and according to tradition this is where the mythical craftsman had his workshop.

Narrow cobbled streets run up from the harbour into the town. The old-fashioned houses perch one above the other against a steep cliff, with panoramic views out to sea. The village stands to the west of a small but fertile plain formed by the Amarianos or Platys river, which flows into the sea to the east of the village.

In antiquity, the site of the village was occupied by a coastal settlement called Soulia or Soulena, the port for ancient Syvritos. The goddess Artemis was worshipped at a temple here. The city was destroyed by the Saracens in 640 AD. When the old religion was succeeded by Christianity, a church of Christ in Peace ('galini') was erected on the foundations of the temple of Artemis. The town cemetery has a church of the Dormition of the Virgin, which was once a monastery church. According to one version of the story, it is to this church —and its male saint— that the village

owes its name, which ought properly to be Ayios Galinis. However, the name might also be derived from ancient Greek words meaning 'peaceful harbour'. Archaeological investigation of the seabed has brought to light a Roman shipwreck of the 3rd century AD, from which were taken figurines, lanterns, busts and copper utensils which can now be seen in the Archaeological Museum at Rethymno. From Ayia Galini there are frequent excursions by sea to Preveli, Plakias, Frangokastelo and Chora Sfakion.

We take the road which will return us to Rethymno. After 5 km there is a turning, left, for th village of **Melambes**. This settlement stands between Mt Kedros and Mt Vouvala, at an altitude of 570 metres.

The road continues through the village and rejoins the main road to Rethymno. This is an

Ayia Galini, on its hillside, looks out over the Libyan Sea. To the right, the fine beach at the estuary of the Amarianos river.

idyllic run, through verdant villages, and it soon leads to **Spili**, the chief town of the Eparchy of Ayios Vasileios.

Spili stands on a rise above the southwest foothills of Mt Kedros. It has numerous streams and is in a thickly-wooded area, where plane trees are very common. The village is an ideal spot for relaxation. In its little square, there are 25 water-spouts in the shape of lions' heads, from whose mouths cool water pours out. From the square, quaint alleyways lead to the upper village, which has pretty houses, courtyards full of flowers and a panoramic view. The little cave ('spilia') called Skisma, at Peristere, has given its name to the village as a whole.

Spili has old churches to the Sts Theodore, St George and the Transfiguration, with exceptionally fine wall-paintings of the damned.

Cool water runs without ceasing from the 25 spouts in the pretty square of the village of Spili.

3. Kourtaliotiko Gorge, Preveli Monastery, Plakias

In Rethymno, our road starts on the eastern side of the Municipal Gardens, heading south towards the higher ground in the centre of the Prefecture. As we climb, the landscape is bare and rocky. However, the view down to Rethymno with the Fortezza and the blue sea which embraces it, is marvellous. We soon run into olive groves and oak forests, and at 11 km arrive at the village of **Armeni**. This pretty village, at 380 m. above sea level, was first settled in the year 961 by Armenians who served in the army of the Byzantine Emperor Nicephorus Phocas which liberated Crete from the Arabs.

At **19 km** we come to a fork. The road to the right leads to the village of Ayios Vasileios and the Kotsyfou gorge. Straight on goes to Spili.

21 km. We turn off the main road for Spili and Ayia Galini and head right, for the Kourtaliotiko Gorge.

23 km Koxare: After the village, the road travels through the impressive **Kourtaliotiko gorge**, formed by the mountains of Kouroupa (984 m) and Xiro Oros (904 m). The gorge begins in Koxare village and continues along the course of the Kourtaliotis river. When a strong wind is blowing, it whistles strangely among the recesses in the rocks; since the noise produced is a kind of rattling ('kourtala' in the local dialect), it gave the river and the gorge their name. The gorge is narrow, grand and wildly beautiful. On its bare sides are numerous springs and caves. The Kourtaliotis river which flows through it rises at five big springs (to the left of the road) which form a waterfall 40 metres high. Today there is a church to St Nicholas in the gorge, together with a little chapel to St George.

We continue, passing through the attractive village of **Asomatos** (altitude 230 m) and at 33 km from Rethymno come to a turning (left) for the historic **Preveli Monastery**. The road is surfaced at first, but soon degenerates into a track. However, the beauty of the landscape more than compensates for any discomfort.

The **Lower Preveli Monastery** appears quite suddenly out of the greenery to the west of the Kourtaliotikos river. It stands by a bridge over the river. Today, the monastery is deserted. Its main church is to John the Baptist, and its belfry bears the date 1594.

A further 3 km brings us to the **Upper Monastery**, which is the more important foundation today. The main church is dedicated to St John the Divine and the bell-tower is dated 1629. The monastery stands on a rocky site with such a fine view that many visitors come to admire that alone.

According to tradition, the name 'Prevelis', derives from a feudal lord of that name who dedicated the monastery and its church of John the Baptist to his feudal estate. The foundation was established in the 16th or early 17th century, and the double-aisled main church was erected in 1836, under the Venetians. It was destroyed in 1866 and restored in 1911. The current abbot's quarters were built in 1900, together with 20 new cells, and the old abbot's quarters were converted into a guesthouse. The monastery served as a base during all the struggles of the Cretans to gain their independence, and in more recent times it was used as an escape route for Allied troops on their way to Egypt after the fall of Crete to the Germans.

Inside the Monastery is a gold crucifix incorporating pieces of the True Cross and precious stones, which is regarded as miraculous. The museum contains books, vestments and, property registers and there is also a library.

From the Lower Preveli Monastery, a path leads down through an idyllic landscape to the coast near the point where the Kourtaliotikos river runs into the sea. *Here the river forms a little lagoon surrounded with palm trees before joining its waters with those of the sea.* The gorge is worth exploring along the river-bank path. The scenery is exotic, with the palm trees all around and the green waters of the river flowing quietly or more rapidly through pools or over little waterfalls. The gorge ends at the beautiful beach, with rocks to the right and left and crystal-clear water.

From Asomatos the road continues west to **Myrthio**. Standing at an altitude of 200 metres, this village has a fine view over Plakias Bay, 4 km away.

The historic Preveli Monastery.

A wonderful secluded beach at the end of the Kourtaliotiko Gorge.

village at a height of 280 metres above sea level. From here on, we drive through outstanding scenery, with a view out to sea. We come to **Ano Rodakino**, a picturesque upland village which forms part of the general Sfakia area. It is built amphitheatrically among olive trees. The road then runs down to **Kato Rodakino**, with a good beach, and along for a further 2 km before coming to the excellent beach at **Korakas**. The road then continues along the south coast to Chora Sfakion. The other road from the Myrthio crossroads turns north east and leads to the end of the Kotsyfou gorge.

The **Kotsyfou Gorge** is formed by the mountains of Kouroupas and Kryoneritis. In many ways, the gorge resembles the Samaria gorge on a smaller scale, and the passage through it is most attractive. The entrance of the gorge is near the upland village of **Ayios Ioannis** (480 m). The road then continues to **Ayios Vasileios**, and then returns to the road to Rethymno.

Now the road runs downhill, and we reach the pretty coastal village of **Plakias**, on the bay of the same name. This is the one of the most beautiful spots on the whole south coast of Crete. Until just a few years ago, Plakias was a sleepy fishing village with a few houses around a shady square. Now, thanks to its sandy beach (1,500 metres long) and the mountain which, like a stage set, towers behind it, it has become a busy resort. Its mild and dry climate make it an ideal spot for off-season holidays.

To the east of Plakias is the coastal settlement of **Damioni**, on a pretty cove.

From Myrthio, the road to the left leads to **Sellia**, an attractive

The pretty bay of Plakias, on the southern shore of Crete.

4. Perama, Melidoni, Anoyeia, Idaean Cave

From Rethymno, we take the Old National Road for Herakleio reaching **Stavromenos**. In this coastal village, which has a good beach, the Old National Road crosses the new highway before reaching Perama. **Perama** is the chief town in the Eparchy of Mylopotamos, and it owes its name to the fact that it is situated on a river crossing ('perama'). Today, it has developed into a major commercial centre for the surrounding area. At the same time, it lies at the heart of a communications network, with roads leaving here for all parts of the district.

From Perama, we head north east. The road is surfaced and the pleasant route, with views over the plain, leads to the **Melidoni** or **Yerontospilio cave**, which is near the village of the same name. In Minoan times, the cave was a place of worship and tablets and a double axe have been found there. Among the deities worshipped were the giant Talos, to whom, according to the myths, King Minos entrusted the implementation of the laws, Hermes Talaios and Zeus Talaios.

In modern times, the most important event was the suffocation in the cave of 370 villagers who had taken shelter there. The Turks set fire to various materials and threw them into the entrance of the cave when the villagers refused to surrender, and so they choked to death on the smoke. Their bones have been preserved in mausoleum near the cave.

The entrance to the cave is reached up an easy staircase and then a path. Inside there are a number of chambers and a fine selection of stalactites and stalagmites.

From Perama, a surfaced road leads south to **Margarites**, a village which was important in Venetian times, **Prine**, an attractive village and ends at **Eleutherna**. It was a city-state of importance in Classical and Roman times.

From Perama the route leads east. After the village of **Mourtziana**, there is a turning south from the Old National Road for Garazo, Axos and Anoyeia.

The village of **Axos** and the land around it village is very fertile; there is abundant water and the climate is good. The village, in the midst of which is a spring with crystal-clear water, is built on the site of the ancient city of Axos or Oaxos. Oaxos stood on the side of a hill, on a number of terraced levels, and it had a well-fortified acropolis. Its port was at Astali, on the bay where Bali stands today. The city was rich and powerful and continued to thrive under the Romans and Byzantium. It issued its own coins, which showed the head of Apollo or Artemis. In the Roman period it continued to mint coins. Of the 46 churches in the area in Byzantine times, only nine have survived.

When the inhabitants of Axos were persecuted by the Venetians, many of them fled eastwards and founded a new village, the Axika Anoyeia or Xinganoyeia. **Anoyeia**, as the village is more simply known today lies on the north slopes of Mt Ida, on the side of a rise known as Armi. It is to this site that it owes its name, which means 'high place'. The village is one of the major handicraft and cottage industry centres in Crete. The goods produced are of extremely high quality, with motifs unique to the village. Woven and embroidered articles are the most popular with visitors. It was here that Greece's first women's co-operative was set up. Anoyeia

also produces fine singers and lyre-players.

The village stands on three different levels. The road from Axos brings us to the first level, the idyllic Perachori, with its plane trees and crystal-clear spring. After this, a wide bend uphill leads to Armi, the centre of Anoyia, the level first settled by the inhabitants of Axos, and the third level, the attractive Metochi.

The people of this village differ from the other Cretans — even from those of nearby areas. The centuries of almost complete isolation up on the mountain mean that they have preserved their traditions in dress, custom and dialect. Their language contains many Ancient Greek words, particularly those to do with the pastoral occupations. However, they are notably hospitable and make a great fuss over their visitors — in a manner rather reminiscent of the *Odyssey,* when Odysseus is received with such warmth at the court of Alcinous. Here, too, in bygone days games, feasts and other celebrations would be held in honour of visitors, in the square of St John with its 12th century church.

Anoyeia took part in all of Crete's struggles for liberation. Under the Turks, it was forever in revolt. In World War II it was a major centre for the resistance movement. Here, in 1944, the guerillas kept the German General von Kreipe prisoner before smuggling him out to Africa. In retaliation, the Germans killed all the men they could find in the village and burned down all the buildings with the exception of the church of St John. Anoyeia was rebuilt after the Occupation.

Every summer there is a festival of the arts.

The proud village of Anoyeia stands high on the northern side of Crete.

From Methochi, a passable road climbs up the side of Mt Ida. At Zomythos, about 6 km along the road, recent excavations have brought to light a Minoan villa. After a drive of about 20 km, we come out above the barren but impressive **Nida plateau**, where there is a pavilion run by the NTOG. This is a good spot to rest, enjoying a piece of 'mizithra' (cheese) from Anoyeia or perhaps some spit-roasted goat.

The climb continues along a steep path which leads to the **Idaean Cave** or, as the local shepherds call it, 'the shepherd girl's cave', at a height of 1,538 metres. West of the cave, a skiing centre is currently being constructed. This was a shrine from prehistoric times until the Roman period, and a place of study of mystical doctrines.

The cave entrance is on a spacious slab of rock where there is a carved rectangular altar. The slab is surrounded by a low wall, sloping amphitheatrically, which is also hewn out of the rock. Next to the entrance was a larch on which pilgrims hung their votive offerings before entering the cave. Inside, there were three chambers and the sanctuary. The second chamber acted as the sanctum of the shrine, where the cult statues were placed. Initiation of the faithful took place in the depths of the cave, in the sanctuary. Steps carved in the rock have been excavated all round the cave and copper statuettes have been found.

Exploration of the cave is quite difficult, because the sloping entrance is covered with snow even into the summer. Inside, objects made of bone and ivory, iron weapons and tools, copper figurines and idols, utensils (trays, tripods and kettles) and votive offerings of shields showing hunting scenes dating from the 8th-7th century BC have been discovered. All are on display in Hall XIX of the Herakleio Archaeological Museum. The finds show us that man was using the cave for the purposes of worship as far back as late Neolithic times.

According to the myths, Rhea brought her son Zeus here in order to hide him from his father Kronos, who was afraid that Zeus would rob him of his heavenly power. To trick Kronos into believing he had eaten Zeus, Rhea swaddled a stone and gave it to him. In the cave, the nymphs Adracteia and Ida nurtured the infant on milk from the goat Amaltheia and wild honey. Outside, the Kouretes danced the Pyrrhicheios war dance and banged their swords on their shields whenever the baby cried, so that Kronos could not hear him.

From Axos a turning to the right leads to the village of **Zoniana**, which owes its name to the soldiers of the Byzantine emperor Nicephorus Phocas. Near the village is the superb **Sendoni Cave**. The scenery is most spectacular. The cave too, is spacious and impressive. The interior is divided into labyrinthine corridors, adorned with stalactites, stalagmites, thick columns and cave pearls.

We continue through the village of **Livadeia**. The village is sited in the midst of a plain of olive trees, vineyards and carobs. Livadeia was on this site as far back as the 13th century, as witnessed by the church of the Annunciation which stands there. We pass through these last villages among the foothills of Mt Ida and make our way back to Perama.

5. Panormos, Bali, Herakleio

From Rethymno a surfaced road leads in 22 km to the coastal village of **Panormos**. The village is built on a fine and densely-vegetated site between two bays, and it has developed into a notable tourist resort. It also acts as a centre for trade and fishing in the area. It is believed to stand on the site of ancient Panormos, which was the port of Eleutherna.

We now take the new National Road for Herakleio. As we travel east, at 33 km takes us down to the pretty fishing village of **Bali**. The village stands at the head of a little bay, on the site of ancient Astale, port of Axos. The heights around the bay form small valleys and little coves. Thanks to its natural position, which is protected from the north west wind, and also to its fine pebble beach, Bali is an excellent place for swimming.

Once, Bali was noted for its beekeeping, and that is perhaps the origin of its name, which in Turkish means 'honey', or 'place of honey'.

We return to the National Road, which continues to the east and passing through the picturesque village of **Sises**, arrives at Herakleio. At about the level of Ayia Pelagia there is an excellent panoramic view of Herakleio and its bay.

The sheltered bay of Bali is an invitation to come in swimming.

THE PREFECTURE OF HERAKLEIO

The Prefecture of Herakleio lies between Mt Psiloritis and the Lasithiotika Mountains and is the largest administrative division of Crete. It has an area of 2,641 square kilometres and a population of approximately 250,000. The island's commerce, farming, stock-breeding and such industry as it has are all concentrated here. The area is full of contradictions; there are peaceful and fertile plains of considerable size (the largest being that of Messara, followed by that of Malevizi), and high and imposing mountains, sometimes bare and sometimes smothered in a riot of cypresses and holm oak, swept by breezes which bear the aroma of the thousands of herbs. In between lie hills covered with fruit trees: cherries, chestnuts, walnuts, date palms and even banana trees. And along the coast are inviting sandy beaches and secret coves where the water is crystal-clear.

Both the coastal and the inland parts of the Prefecture have been inhabited without interruption since prehistoric times, and so the area is the richest in Crete in terms of archaeological sites, with the marvellous Minoan palaces at Knossos, Phaestos and Mallia and even the town of Herakleio itself, which can offer a striking combination of medieval and more modern buildings, historic sites and traditional districts.

From the point of view of tourist facilities, the Prefecture has a complete range of services. Large hotel units and tourist businesses are to be found everywhere, and there is plenty of choice of comfortable accommodation and high-quality services.

There are daily car-ferry sailings from Herakleio to Piraeus. Herakleio international airport is fully capable of meeting the considerable air traffic demands. There are domestic flights to Athens, Thessaloniki, Rhodes, Mykonos, Paros and Santorini. Inside the Prefecture, there are town and long-distance (KTEL) bus services to all the villages, beaches and archaeological sites. In the summer, there are ferry sailings to the Cyclades, while cruise liners operating out of Venice link Herakleio to Limassol in Cyprus and Haifa in Israel.

Herakleio

1. Kule (Venetian Fortress)
2. Venetian Harbour
3. Port Authority
4. Buses to Lasithi
5. Commercial School
6. Archaeological Museum
7. Tourist Organisation (DOG)
8. Eleftherias Square
9. Olympic Airways
10. Public Garden
11. Ayios Markos
12. Venizelou Square
13. Morosini Fountain
14. Loggia
15. Ayios Titos
16. Telecommunications Organisation (OTE)
17. The El Greco Park
18. Historical Museum
19. Ayia Triada
20. Ayia Ekaterini
21. The Cathedral of Ay. Minas
22. Kornarou Square

The city of Herakleio

Including its suburbs, the city of Herakleio has today a population in excess of 110,000.

Herakleio has been the capital of Crete since 1972 and is the island's economic capital, with extensive commercial and industrial sectors. Most visitors to Crete arrive at its harbour or its airport, which is the island's largest. As the ship sails into the harbour, approaching visitors will see the large stone head of Zeus on the sacred mountain Yiouchtas, the large Venetian fortress and, next to it, a modern tourist pavilion. Both stand on the top of a hill and behind them the massif of Mt Ida rises menacingly. This is usually the first contact and acquaintance of visitors with Crete.

The city itself consists of two parts: the new town, with its modern shops, parks, and busy squares, and the old town, with its Venetian fountains, the Loggia, its markets and its alleys: the present and the past. The alleys in the old town often bear historic dates as names: 1821 St, 25 August St, 1866 St. Only a very few of them are wide enough to take motor traffic, and even then only just.

The city and its suburbs have large numbers of modern, comfortable hotels capable of accommodating more than 4,000 visitors. Outside the town, too, large hotel complexes stretch along the fine beaches.

In Minoan times, the site of the modern city was occupied by a little harbour belonging to Knossos. When the Greeks, moving south, reached Crete, they called this harbour Herakleia and that was the name by which it was known in Classical and Roman times. Nonetheless, during those periods it had no historical significance.

It was not until 824 AD, when Crete was taken by the Saracens, that Herakleio acquired some military and economic importance. The medieval city, which was then known as Chandax —a name it kept throughout the Byzantine period— was fortified by the Arabs with a deep moat and strong walls and became an almost invulnerable stronghold. From it, the Saracens set out on their pirate raids, and Chandax market contained a slave bazaar which was among the largest in the eastern Mediderranean.

In 961 Nicephorus Phocas, who later became Emperor of Byzantium, retook Chandax for the Empire with his army. For the Arabs, the fall of Chandax meant the end of their rule in Crete. The town was rebuilt and provided with even stronger fortifications and a new wall starting from the site where the Xenia hotel stands today and running down to the harbour by way of the Archaeological Museum.

Crete was taken by the Venetians in 1210 and Chandax, or Candia as they called it, became the island's capital. In fact, at that time the whole of Crete was known as Candia. In the four centuries during which the Venetians ruled Crete, many impressive houses, churches and administrative buildings were erected in Herakleio, and fountains were set up to supply water and decorate the city.

After the fall of Constaninople to the Turks in 1453, Candia flourished, since many artists, intellectuals and men of wealth and position sought refuge there. The city began to spread outside its Byzantine walls and so a new defensive ring had to be built. These are the walls which have survived down to the present, and whose building took more than 100 years. The new walls were more than three kilometres in length and had seven bastions. The four great gates were built between 1565 and 1587 and are: the Old Gate (which led to the break-water and was demolished in 1898), the Lazaretto Gate, the New Gate and the *Chania Gate*, which is also called the Pantokratoras Gate. Particular attention was paid to the town's defences on the seaward side.

The strength of Candia's fortifications was amply demonstrated by the siege of 1648-1669, when they resisted

the attacks of the Turks for 21 years: the rest of Crete had submitted to the invaders as early as 1645. In the end, the Venetians were forced to call a truce, and Francesco Morosini, the last Venetian commissioner for Crete, was able to negotiate with the Turks the unimpeded withdrawal of himself and his men.

When the Turks took over the city they soon succeeded in changing its atmosphere. Ruined buildings were repaired and new ones erected, the walls were put right and churches were converted into mosques. Year by year, the face of the town changed. Many Greek Christians were forced to leave, and before long Candia was a thoroughly Oriental town. Even the name changed: now it was known as Megalo Kastro ('big castle') or just Kastro.

The Venetian Loggia.

The Chania Gate.

The Kule (frortress) which protects the Venetian harbour.

On the departure of the Turks, the city went back to its ancient roots, being called Herakleio after the Herakleia of antiquity. It changed aspect once more, as large parts of the old town were flattened by earthquake and others demolished to make way for new buildings.

In the course of its long history, Herakleio has been destroyed and rebuilt many times, but the 'development' which has occurred since the Second World War has been particularly rough-and-ready and anarchic. Nonetheless, there are still many sights to see, and a walk round the town will satisfy even the most demanding visitor.

A visit to the old town should begin in Eleftherias Square. To the north of the square is the Herakleio Archaeological Museum, with its unique collection of Minoan treasures. This was once the site of the convent of St Francis. The offices of the NTOG stand opposite the Museum. Daidalou St, a narrow and bustling thoroughfare lined with restaurants and shops, begins off the west of the square and leads to Eleftheriou Venizelou Square. Parallel to Daidalou St runs Dikaiosinis St; on the left-hand side of this are the Venetian barracks, rebuilt by the Turks. Today they house prefectural departments and the Tourist Police. Dikaiosinis St leads to 1866 St, where the vegetable market and the town's butcher's shops are situated. Herakleio market, full of noise and colour, is very picturesque, and the range of produce on sale is startling. At the end of Dikaiosinis St we turn right, and after 50 metres emerge in Eleftheriou Venizelou Square.

Here there are abundant cafes, restaurants and souvenir shops.

During the Venetian period, this square and the streets which surround it were the centre of the town. It also holds the *Morosini Fountain*, or 'the Lions' as the local call it. This is the emblem of the city of Herakleio, and it was erected in 1628 by Francesco Morosini, who was then commissioner of the island. The fountain was the termination of the city's aqueduct, which brought water to Herakleio from Mt Yiouchtas, 15 km. away. The four lions date from the 14th century. The reliefs which decorate the fountain show scenes from Greek mythology: Tritons, nymphs and dolphins.

If we head north from Eleftheriou Venizelou Square, we will find ourselves in the little Kallergon Square. Here stands the *Venetian Loggia*, a building in the Italian Renaissance style initially erected in 1623-1628 and used as a club for the Venetian nobility. This wonderful building, the finest constructed by the Venetians in Herakleio, was destroyed by bombing during the Second World War and has been restored to its original form. Today it houses Herakleio Town Hall.

Directly behind the Loggia is the Byzantine *church of St Titus*. In Turkish times, this was converted into a mosque (the Vezir-Cami) in honour of the Grand Vizier Ciopruli, who took the city. In 1856 the church collapsed in a severe earthquake and it was not restored until 1922. The relics of St Titus, who is the patron saint of Crete, are kept inside.

From here, 25 August St, which is the town's commercial centre, with banks and travel agencies, runs down to the old Venetian harbour, where yachts and fishing-boats now moor.

The *Venetian harbour* was protected by the *Grand Kule*, a squat two-storey fortress which is still standing despite the damage done by the waves and the centuries. The Kule is an impressive example of Venetian military engineering, despite its Turkish name. It was first erected in the 13th century, but in 1303 it was destroyed by earthquake. The building we see today is that erected in 1523-1540. There are remnants of a minaret to remind us of the Turkish period, and the view of the harbour from the walls of the fortress is striking.

The Morosini fountain.

The Cathedral of St Minas

A further walk through the town also starts from Eleftheriou Venizelou Square. The market street take us down to Kornarou Square, where stands the *Bembou Fountain*. Built by the architect Bembo in 1588, it incorporates fragments of a Roman sarcophagus and a headless Roman statue.

The kiosk next to it was once a Turkish fountain. It was restored in 1982 and is now one of the most attractive cafes in Herakleio.

To the west of Kornarou Square stands the *Cathedral of St Minas* (1862-1895), the largest church on Crete. Inside are six icons by the great Cretan icon-painter Michail Damaskinos, who lived in the 16th century and was among the teachers of Domenico Theotokopoulos (El Greco).

The *Venetian Walls*, work on the construction of which began in 1462, protect the city on three sides. They were built to plans by Michele Senmicheli, one of the most famous architects of military frotifications. The thickness of the walls is as much as 60 metres in some places, and the moat, which can still be seen at some points, was between 20 and 60 metres broad. The walls were completed by 1550-1560.

The top of the walls can be reached only by the staircase leading up to the *Martinengo Bastion*, which is the highest point in the town. The view over Herakleio is panoramic.

Here, too, is the *tomb of Nikos Kazantzakis*, a square monument of large stones with a roof and a wooden cross. The simple, white plaque bears the words of the great author: *"I have no hopes and no fears, I am free"*.

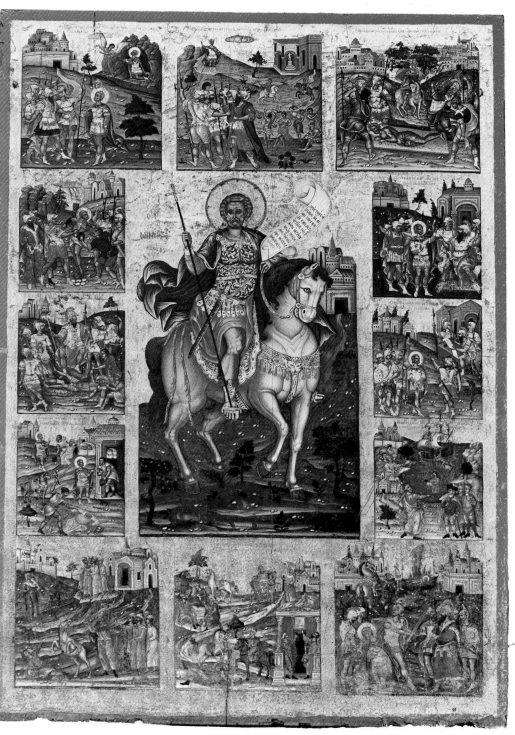

St Minas in twelve scenes from his life and martyrdom.
A portable icon from the little church of St Minas, painted by Y. Kastrofylakas, 1738.

"The Adoration of the Magi", Michail Damaskinos, 16th century.

The **Museum of Byzantine Icons** is housed in the church of St Catherine, built in 1555. During the 16th and 17th centuries, the school which was based in the church played an important part in the intellectual life of the island. Today, the Museum contains collection of works of Christian art from all over Crete. There are icons (including some superb specimens of the Cretan school of painting), wall-paintings and ecclesiastical vessels.

One of the most representative works of the Museum —and one of Damaskinos' finest creations— is "The Adoration of the Magi", dating from the 16th century. The figuration is quite un-Byzantine, yet the icon succeeds in blending the Greek and the Italian traditions and in expressing the style and artistic genius of the painter in all its majesty.

Of the museums of Herakleio, the Archaeological Museum is unique of its kind and is by itself worth a journey to Crete. However, because of its size and importance and the wealth of its exhibits, we have left the description of it to the end of this chapter, just before the trip to Knossos, with which the Museum is so closely bound up. The Historical Museum is also very interesting, because its wonderful collections cast quite a different light on the history of the island. The Museum of Byzantine Icons, too, is of importance, with its works of Christian art.

The **Herakleio Historical Museum** is housed in a neo-Classical mansion. Its collections include items which are important for the history, religion and ethnology of Crete from Early Christian times down to the present. They include sculptures, inscriptions, copper engravings, Byzantine icons, examples of local costume, furniture, woven goods, documents, wood-carvings and musical instruments.

The Historical Museum has a special hall devoted to Nikos Kazantzakis, with his books, manuscripts, personal effects and the desk at which he worked.

Of course, Herakleio has far more to show than historic buildings and museums. It also has fine beaches, for example all of which are accessible by town bus. Using urban transport, it is possible to reach the beaches of Lintos (2 km.), Ammoudara (5 km.) and Linoperamata (7 km.). These beaches lie to the west of the town. To the east, the town buses run to Nea Alikarnassos (3 km.), Amnisos (7 km.) and Karterou (8 km.). The town buses depart from Eleftherias Square. The beaches at Amnisos and Karterou are generally reckoned to be the best in the vicinity.

Views of Herakleio from the Venetian harbour.

The **Archaeological Museum** contains an incredible collection of Minoan art works arranged in 20 large galleries. These exhibits cover the whole of Cretan civilisation from the Neolithic period to the end of the Helleno-Roman age, and there are finds not only from Knossos but from the whole of Crete (mostly the eastern and central parts). Of particular interest are the jewellery, the wall-paintings from the palace of Knossos and the pottery, which is of rare beauty. Some of the finest Minoan treasures, such as the 16th century BC vase of the Harvesters, came from the archaeological site of Ayia Triada.

All visitors to the Archaeological Museum, are charmed by the beauty of the statuettes. *One of the most famous is the faience statuette of the Goddess with the Snakes, symbol of fertility.*

Before entering the Museum, perhaps it would be as well to have in mind a few points about **Minoan art** in general.

To judge from their art at least, it would seem that from very early times the Cretans

A clay libation vessel, 1500 BC.

were lovers of nature, elegance and beauty. Their art-works are usually small in size. They appear to have had a particular weakness for painting, and all their wall-paintings stand out for their ability to capture motion, which is rendered with delicacy and vigour. The spiral is the basic decorative motif.

Minoan art falls into three basic periods: Early Minoan (3600-2100 BC), Middle Minoan (2100-1600 BC), and Late Minoan (1600-1200 BC), each of which is further sub-divided into three shorter periods. The golden age of Minoan art, which lasted about 100 years, fell during the Late Minoan period.

Some idea of what the people of the Minoan age must have looked like can be gained from their portrayals in paintings and sculptures. The men seem to have worn light clothing, their dress consisting only of a multi-coloured piece of cloth around the waist, although there are depictions of officials in richly-worked cloaks and headgear. Tight belts emphasised the slim waists of both men and women. The women of Crete, light and mobile as the wall-paintings show them to us, took great care with dressing their hair, decorating the arrangement on top with jewels and multi-coloured ribbons. Their dresses were very low cut (or perhaps it would be more accurate to say that they went bare-breasted) and the skirts, drawn in at the waist, hung down low.

The women of Minoan Crete seem to have been emancipated; in the wall-paintings they are shown watching religious ceremonies, dances and games in a position of absolute equality with the men.

Apart from these wall-paintings, the Minoans were highly-skilled workers in stone, ivory and precious stones, with a particular trend towards the faithful representation of reality. In many cases what we have are copies in more common materials (for the times) of genuine items which have been lost and which would have been in metal. Miniatures, too, were of the highest level of quality, as we can see primarily in the jewellery of this distant age and also in its pottery.

The pottery of Early Minoan times consists principally of rhytons, water jugs and long-stemmed goblets. Many of these have taken the names of the sites where they were found. Most are red-form against a background in the light natural colour of the clay, though some have light-coloured designs on a dark ground.

The smaller works of art from tholos tombs rich in archaeological finds also date from this period. Among these are seals of ivory and semi-precious stones bearing the figures of animals, stone pots from Mochlos and clay statuettes of goddesses. *One of the most valuable exhibits in the Museum is the black steatite bull's head rhyton,* which would have been used for libations.

The finest gold jewellery (diadems, necklaces, etc.) consists of leaves, rosettes and animal figures.

A rhyton from the palace at Zakro, 1450 BC.

Among the most famous exhibits in the Museum are the multi-coloured egg-shell pots from a cave at Kamares. Dated to the Middle Minoan period (2000-1776 BC), they usually show natural and maritime scenes. The principal decorative motif is the octupus, whose tentacles weave in among seaweed and shells. When this motif first appears the decorative outcome was wonderfully delicate, but with the passage of time it became corrupted into simple copies and by Late Minoan III the tentacles have acquired the shape of nooses. The way in which these pots were decorated, with their fascinating colours, gave the name 'Kamares ware' to all the pottery from that particular period.

The statuettes of goddesses, such as the snake goddess, and the pots with relief decoration (showing scenes from everyday life with great vigour), which include the so-called Chieftain cup (which shows three officials reporting to a young prince), the Harvester Vase and the Boxer Vase with its four bands of decoration, also date from this period. The gold jewellery, such as the necklace with the duck from Knossos, or the necklace with the lion from Ayia Triada, are testimony to the level of sophistication which miniature work and the goldsmith's art had reached in Minoan Crete.

The egg-shell Kamares ware found in a cave on Mt Ida was so sought-after at the time that the Minoans exported it to the other Aegean islands and all along the coasts of the Mediterranean. There are also superb crystal vases from the Late Minoan period.

The galleries of the Museum are organised on a thematic basis and their numbering reflects the dates of the exhibits.

The exhibits indicated briefly below are of particular interest and should on no account be missed when touring the Museum.

Gallery II: Finds from the Early Palace period (2000-1700 BC). Kamares ware with multi-coloured decoration.

Gallery III: Finds from the Early Palace period. Case 41: the famous Phaestos Disc, with writing in a script that has not as yet been deciphered.

Gallery IV: Exhibits from the Late Palace period (1700-1450 BC), found at the palaces of Knossos and Phaestos. Case 50: two statuettes of the Minoan snake goddess. Case 56: Ivory figures relating to the bull-leaping ceremony. The figures are shown in the act of leaping.

Gallery VII: Finds from the Late Palace period. Case 94: the incomparable Harvester Vase, from Ayia Triada. The farmers return home, in a procession of thanksgiving for a good harvest. Case 101: gold necklace with two bees.

Gallery VIII: Late Palace period finds from Kato Zakros. Case 111: a rhyton in the shape of a temple.

Gallery XIII: Minoan sarcophagi from a variety of all periods.

Gallery XX: Sculpture from the Greek and Roman periods.

Upper floor: Minoan frescoes (wall-paintings) from Knossos, Amnisos and Ayia Triada.

Gallery XIV: case 171: the famous Ayia Triada sarcophagus decorated with frescoes — one of the finest examples of Minoan painting.

One the walls are the incomparable frescoes of the Toreador, the Prince of the Lilies from Amnisos and the Wild Cat from Ayia Triada.

Gallery XV: La Parisienne, a wonderful fresco from the Knossos Palace. Fragments of a relief showing acrobats.

Gallery XVI: the fresco of the monkey gathering saffron in a field, and the Blue Bird fresco.

Gallery XVIII: the Yamalakis collection. Case 175: the Neolithic fertility goddess.

A clay Kamares pot from Phaestos, 1800 BC.

A clay Kamares krater, from the palace at Phaestos, 1800 BC.

Bull-leaping: the ceremony of bull-leaping and bull-fighting appears to have been among the Minoans' favourite spectacles. The ceremony ('tavrokathapsia') was held in one of the palace courtyards and the residents, men and women, are sure to have watched with great enthusiasm.

The bull would rush snorting into the appointed area, while the nearly naked boys and girls would throw themselves in its path, seize its horns and leap high into the air over its head. After

turning a somersault in the air, they would land gracefully on the back of the enraged beast. Another vault with a somersault would land them back on the ground, in the safe arms of their partner. Of course, there would often have been occasions on which the furious bull would attack while the young people were defenceless, and then the arena would be stained with the blood of these brave boys and girls.

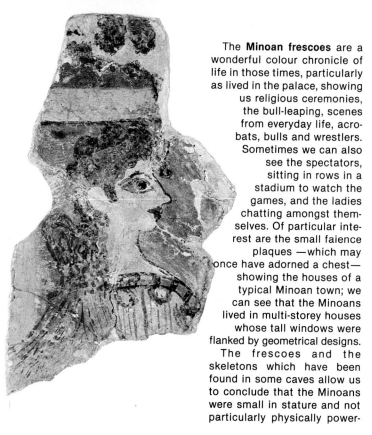

The **Minoan frescoes** are a wonderful colour chronicle of life in those times, particularly as lived in the palace, showing us religious ceremonies, the bull-leaping, scenes from everyday life, acrobats, bulls and wrestlers. Sometimes we can also see the spectators, sitting in rows in a stadium to watch the games, and the ladies chatting amongst themselves. Of particular interest are the small faience plaques —which may once have adorned a chest— showing the houses of a typical Minoan town; we can see that the Minoans lived in multi-storey houses whose tall windows were flanked by geometrical designs.

The frescoes and the skeletons which have been found in some caves allow us to conclude that the Minoans were small in stature and not particularly physically power-ful, but that they must have been very quick movers. They were fond of amusements and took very little interest in the art of war. In fact, there are no scenes of war or hunting in any Minoan art work, and it would appear that there were no other wild animals on Crete than polecats, wild cats, weasels and wild goats (which, of course, have survived down to the present).

Apart from the scenes from everyday life, many of the frescoes show landscapes and life at sea — here the famous Dolphin fresco comes to mind.

However, the two most famous frescoes of all show human figures: the Prince with the Lilies, a fragment of a superb fresco which adorned the palace of Knossos, and la Parisienne, a section from a fresco showing a ceremony and including a beautiful young priestess.

La Parisienne and the Blue Ladies, Knossos, 1500 BC.

The wall relief entitled entitled the Prince with the Lilies.

Trips from Herakleio

1. Knossos. 2. Ayia Varvara, Zaros, Vrontisiou Monastery, Kamares. 3. Ayii Deka, Gortyns, Phaestos, Matala. 4. Lentas, Kali Limenes. 5. Archanes, Vathypetro, Apanosifis Monastery. 6. Kasteli, Viannos, Arvi. 7. Tylisos, Fodele, Ayia Pelagia. 8. Amnisos, Chersonisos, Mallia.

1. Knossos

Knossos is, of course, Crete's most famous monument: the largest, strongest and most impressive of the island's Minoan palaces. Knossos is a must for every visitor to Crete. When these ruins were a Minoan palace, they were inhabited by a king, Minos, descendant of the mythical Minos who sprang from the union of Europa and Zeus. Minos was the founder of Cretan naval power, he was the scourge of pirates; he was also a wise legislator and the head of the Minoan religion. Every nine years he went up to the Diktaean Cave to commune with Zeus, his father, and renew his mandate for the next nine years.

Minos is a mixture of myth and history; in the myths, in order to win the throne of Crete, he asked Poseidon to send him a bull, so as to demonstrate to the Cretans that he had been chosen by the gods and that they should accept him as their ruler. He promised to sacrifice the bull to Poseidon afterwards, but broke his promise, letting the god-sent bull graze peacefully in a field while sacrificing an ordinary one to the god. He was to pay dearly for his attempt to hoodwink the god; his wife Pasiphae fell madly in love with the sacred bull and their union produced a monster with the head of a bull

and the body of a man: the Minotaur. Daedalus built the Labyrinth so that the Minotaur could be shut up in it and its rapacity was satisfied by the seven young men and seven maidens whom the Athenians were compelled to send to Crete as tribute each year. Of course, there is some truth lurking behind the myth, which tells us of the power of Crete and of Athens' subjugation to the island power. In addition, in the Labyrinth we find a hint of the number and complexity of the rooms in the palace, where it would be easy for a stranger to lose himself.

This was the famous palace of Knossos, the most ancient and most renowned city of Crete, around which the Minoan civilisation grew and prospered. The site was first inhabited in Neolithic times, around 5000-6000 BC, and this was the first city-state which can be called Greek, home of the first Greek religion and the first Greek art. The Minoans fashioned their own civilisation out of the most valuable elements of previous cultures in Asia and Egypt; in turn, their civilisation acted as the cradle of Western civilisation today.

The palace stands on the hill now known as Kefalas, next to the river Kairatos in the midst of a fertile plain. It had a total area of some 22,000 square metres, and around it stretched a city whose population has been estimated at between 80,000 and 100,000. Its outlets to the sea were at Amnisos and Herakleio, while its territory on Crete extended from Mt Ida to Lyttos. After the glories of the Minoan age, Knossos prospered once again in historical times (8th-6th centuries) and was the leading city on Crete, though by this time it had rivals in Gortyn and Lyttos. In the 3rd century BC it joined the alliance of Cretan cities which cam-

paigned —unsuccessfully— against Lyttos. Later, however, when the Lyttians were off warring elsewhere, the alliance took their city and destroyed it. Knossos was one of the cities which signed the treaty with Eumenes. In 166 BC it allied itself with Gortyn to destroy Raucos, near the modern village of Ayios Myronas. In 69 BC it was taken by the Roman Metellus and, although still important, lost its leading position on the island to Gortyn. In Early Christian times Knossos was the seat of a bishop, later losing this distinction to Raucos. It was finally destroyed by the Arabs; weeds grew over the site and it was forgotten. Under the Venetians, a small village grew up here, by the name Makryteichos ('long wall', from the remains of a wall).

Knossos minted a large variety of coins. Most show the Minotaur holding a stone in its hand. The Labyrinth is also a favourite theme; sometimes it is shown as square and sometimes circular, with the word ΚΝΩΣΙΩΝ. Another theme is the head of Athena, the goddess who founded the dynasty of Knossos, and Demeter is shown to mark the city's pride in its boast of having been the first place where wheat was used as food. However, whatever the motif on one side of the coin, the other always depicted the Labyrinth, the principal Minoan symplol. This was true even in Roman times, when the Roman Consul's head was always shown. Apart from its connection with the mythical home of the Minotaur, the word labyrinth also means 'the house of Labrys' — that is, of the double axe, since labrys is derived from a Lybian word meaning precisely that. The double axe was the most sacred symbol of Minoan religion and as a decorative motif is to be found everywhere in Knossos.

The first archaeologist to work at Knossos was a Greek, Minos Kalokairinos, in 1878, but it was not until 1900, when Sir Arthur Evans arrived on the scene, that excavations were at all systematic. The palace we see today is not the first built on the site (which, like all the other palaces on Crete, was flattened by the earthquake of 1700 BC). It is the second palace, rebuilt after the destruction of the first. Its magnificence marks the resurgence of Minoan Crete in the period until the final catastrophe in around 1400 BC.

The Palace

We enter the archaeological site of the Palace by the *West Court*, where the upward-sloping corridors and the altar bases indicate that this must have been the starting-point for processions. On our right is a bust of Evans, the reconstructor of Knossos. On our left are three *Circular Pits*, as much as five metres deep; at the bottom can be seen the remains of the houses which were built on this site before the palace and were later used as granaries or as dumps for the remains of sacrifices. This latter view is supported by the ceremonial implements and animal bones found there. We follow the corridor south. We enter the palace proper via the *West Entrance*. On the stone base which has survived was a wooden column. This is followed by the guardhouse and a reception room, in which there was a throne. We continue along the narrow *Processional Corridor,* in a souther-ly direction. The corridor takes its name from the frescoes which were found there, showing a procession of hundreds of young men and women bringing offerings to the gods.

Now we enter the palace by the imposing *Propylaeum*, where there were frescoes of a procession of young men carrying vessels. Here too was found the famous *Cup Bearer*, which is in Herakleio Museum today.

We climb the *Grand Staircase*, which was flanked by rows of columns and which led to the upper floor, the *Piano Nobile*, where the official apartments were. At the head of the staircase we pass through an entrance with an antechamber and then into the *Tricolumnar Hall*, where the procession of young men may have ended. To the south was the Treasury. The

The palace of Knossos: the eastern side of the west wing, looking on to the central court (impression).

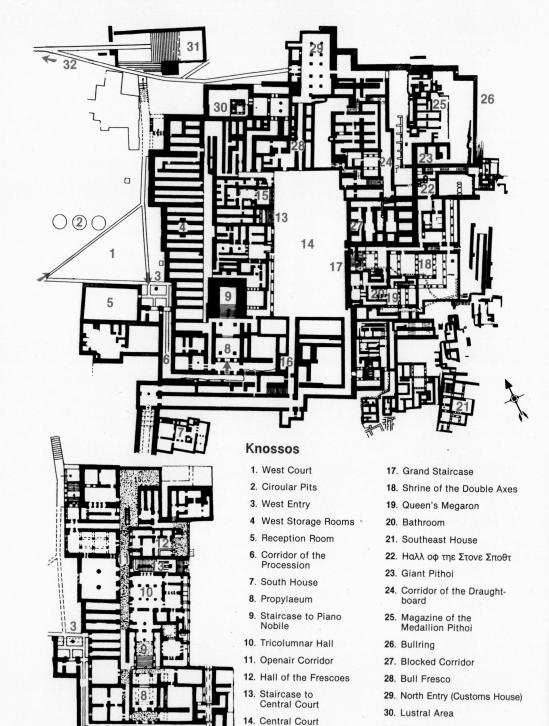

Knossos

1. West Court
2. Ciroular Pits
3. West Entry
4. West Storage Rooms
5. Reception Room
6. Corridor of the Procession
7. South House
8. Propylaeum
9. Staircase to Piano Nobile
10. Tricolumnar Hall
11. Openair Corridor
12. Hall of the Frescoes
13. Staircase to Central Court
14. Central Court
15. Throne Room
16. Prince with the Lilies

17. Grand Staircase
18. Shrine of the Double Axes
19. Queen's Megaron
20. Bathroom
21. Southeast House
22. Ηαλλ οφ τηε Στονε Σποθτ
23. Giant Pithoi
24. Corridor of the Draught-board
25. Magazine of the Medallion Pithoi
26. Bullring
27. Blocked Corridor
28. Bull Fresco
29. North Entry (Customs House)
30. Lustral Area
31. Theatre
32. Paved Road to the Small Palace

Piano Nobile is bisected by the open-air *Long Corridor,* which let light into the rooms on either side of it. After the Corridor, on the left, is the large *Hall of the Two Columns* and a smaller one with six columns, which may have been a shrine. From here we can see the ground-floor store-rooms, where many enormous storage jars for wine, olive oil, grain and honey were found. We now enter the *Hall of the Frescoes,* which is above the Throne Room and communicates with it by a spiral staircase. This hall contains a series of copies of frescoes found in the palace and in a neighbouring house. Here we can admire the *Blue Ladies* and the *Miniature Frescoes* from the cell area, the *Leader of the Blacks* from the House of Frescoes and a whole series of representations of the plant and animal kingdom. On the south side of the Hall of the Frescoes, at right angles to the Long Corridor, a fine broad staircase leads down to the Central Court.

The *Central Court,* which was paved, separates the official chambers on the western side from the private apartments on the east. As in all the Minoan palaces, it is the nucleus of the whole building; it was used for religious ceremonies, athletic performances and contests, and other activities. In addition, it provided light and fresh air for the surrounding rooms. On the western side of the Central Court, under the Hall of the Frescoes, was the *Throne Room,* set amid a group of rooms dating from the Late Minoan period. The Throne Room consists of an antechamber with stone benches (blackened by the fire which destroyed Knossos),

The south Propylaea.

The grand staircase in the east wing.

The Throne-room.

and contains a wooden throne which is a copy of that in the Throne Room itself. Here the archaeologists have placed a large purple limestone vessel. We now come to the *Throne Room* proper, which is protected by a wooden railing. On the north wall is Minos' alabaster throne; hawks, symbols of power, are painted on the walls to the right and left. Directly opposite the throne is a small *Lustral Area.*

In the south west corner of the Central Court, where the processional corridor ends, is a copy of the famous relief fresco called *The Prince with the Lilies,* in its original position. The fresco shows an idealised Minoan royal figure.

The east wing of the Palace stood on a hill, and at some points it must have been five floors in height. This wing is dominated by the *Great Staircase,* with its broad, low steps, one of the greatest works of ancient architecture. It begins about halfway along the eastern side of the Central Court and divides the east wing into its northern section, where the Palace's storerooms and workshops were located, and its south eastern section, where the royal apartments were.

We climb the Great Staircase, with its light-shaft and the columns which lined it, an outstanding example of Minoan engineering. On the east wall of the veranda on the first floor of the *Upper Portico* has been placed a copy of the *Fresco of the Octagonal Shields.* On the ground floor was the main *Hall of the Colonnades.* The shaft here supplied the rooms with light and fresh air. Though a door in the north east side of the Hall of the Colonnades we enter a corridor and turn right, coming to the *Hall of the Double Axes,* so-called because of the frequency with which this motif is repeated on the walls. To the left is the *Outer Chamber of the Double Axes,* where a wooden throne now occupies the place of the original. To the east and south of this hall there were colonnades and light-shafts. We leave the inner hall through a doorway to the south, and after passing along a curving corridor reach the **Queen's Megaron. Over the entrance is a copy of the imposing** *Dolphin Fresco.* On the north west side of this hall is a small room with a bath and a banded column, the *Queen's Bathroom.* To the south west is the *Corridor of the Painted Pithos,* which ends at a *Toilet.* Light comes from an open area called the *Court of the Distaffs.* The eastern wall is the toilet itself, connected to an advanced drainage network, details of which can be seen in the dark corridor which follows. We continue along the corridor, coming to a staircase, on the left, to the upper floors. The corridor brings us back to the Hall of the Colonnades; from here, we continue through the Hall of the Double Axes to come out into the *East Portico* of the Palace. To the east is the *East Bastion* with the interesting *East Entrance,* where there is a complex system for impeding the force of the rainwater as it runs down.

We continue along the paved *Corridor of the Draught-board,* where an inlaid gaming-board was found. To the south east of the Corridor of the Draught-board there is an open court with the upper part of the drain which ended in the Court of the Stone Spout. From here a doorway to the west leads to the *Corridor of the Bays,* whose massive pillars show that there must have been a large hall on the upper floor. We continue, reaching the *Upper Portico* and, on the left, the *Upper Hall of the Double Axes.* The door to the south west leads to the *Upper Queen's Megaron.* The

The Queen's Megaron.

The reconstructed north entrance.

floor-plan here is exactly the same as on the ground floor.

We return to the Central Court and head north, going into the *North Entrance Corridor*. To the east of this were store-rooms, while to the west are the foundations of the oldest part of the Palace, the so-called *Old Cells*. It was above this area that the *Saffrongatherer* and the *Miniature Frescoes* were found. The corridor ends in a hypostyle chamber, the so-called *Customs Post,* to the east of which is the *Northeast Entrance Corridor*. Above the bastions of the corridor are porticoes with friezes in relief.

The western portico, which has been restored, was chosen as the site for the modern copy of the wonderfully lifelike fresco of the Charging Bull, shown against the background of an olive grove. To the west of these porticos is the *North West Proportico,* followed by an *Antechamber* and the *Lustral Area,* where those entering the Palace from this side could be purified.

As we leave the Palace to the north west, we come to the *Theatral Area*. This flat paved area has tiers of seats on its eastern and southern sides, while in the southeast corner

is a raised platform which, it is believed, was the 'royal box'. To the west of the Theatre is the oldest road in Europe: it is paved, and joins up with the main thoroughfare heading north for the *Little Palace*. Along the road also stood the *House of the Frescoes* and the *Armoury*. From the Little Palace, continuing north, we can visit the *Royal Villa* which lies to the north east in the valley behind Knossos. Here the *Partridge Fresco* was found, and here there was also a bridge which facilitated communications with the Palace over the stream.

2. Ayia Varvara, Zaros, Vrontisiou Monastery, Kamares

The Messara road leads south from Herakleio, in the direction of Mires. As we continue, we come at 20 km., to the village of **Neo Venerato**. A side-road to the right goes up to **Venerato**, from which an unsurfaced track goes to the **Paliani Convent**, one of the oldest monestic foundations on Crete. Beside the triple-aisled church is an ancient myrtle tree; at its roots was found an icon of Our Lady, and since then the tree has been revered as holy.

Our attractive run through dense greenery continues to **Ayia Varvara**, at 40 km. The village stands on a site with a panoramic view towards Malevizi. The area around it is green and fertile, and there are abundant orchards and vegetable gardens. It takes its name from the church of St Barbara, a 13th century building which stands in the centre of the village. Ayia Varvara is something of a road junction, as some of the island's most important roads pass through it and intersect there. On a rock at the entrance to the village stands the **Church of the Prophet Elijah**, which is popularly said to be the centre of Crete, in the sense that the north and south coasts are equidistant from it, as are the eastern and western extremities.

As we leave the village, we take the right-hand fork and run downhill across a slope densely planted with fruit trees into the midst of a verdant valley with numerous streams. We soon come to **Panasos**, a very old settlement with a number of early churches which has kept its pre-Hellenic name.

The road climbs once more, up the steep sides of Mt Ida, to the thickly-vegetated village of **Gergeri**, which may owe its name to the tumbling noise ('gargara') made by its many streams. This village is a centre for stockbreeding and handicrafts. A very poor road leads off to the left to the wonderful **Rouva forest**, at an altitude of 1300 m., surrounded by the highest peaks of Mt Ida.

From Gergeri the road continues through the pretty village of **Nivrytos**, which also has a pre-Hellenic name. We then come to **Apano Zaros**, set amid scenery where streams and dense vegetation dominate. The area around the village is very fertile, and there are olive groves and market gardens. Nearby is the Votamos spring, where there are stone fountains and shady plane trees; perhaps of more interest to the hungry traveller, there are two trout farms, whose products can be sampled.

We leave the village and soon come to a turning (right), to the **Vrontisiou Monastery** (1 km.). The monastery stands clinging to the steep slopes of Mt Ida under huge plane trees. It has a panoramic view over the fertile Mesara plain. In former days, the Vrontisiou Monastery was a dependency of the Varsamonerou Monastery. Its double-aisled church, which is dedicated to St Anthony and St Thomas, contains some 14th century wall-paintings. In a corner outside the church, on a stone plaque, is a sun-dial with Roman numerals rather like the one to be seen at Vizari. Near the monastery entrance is a marvellously-crafted 15th century fountain. The relief in the centre of this shows Adam and Eve in Eden, God, and four figures at their feet to symbolise the four rivers of Eden. From the mouths of these figures runs the fountains's refreshing water. The belfry stands, characteristically, at some distance from the church, and has arches in the Western style.

The Vrontisiou Monastery was one of the most important monastic centres in Crete during the final century of Venetian rule. It also became a major centre of learning, where painting and the arts were taught. There is a tradition that the great Cretan painter Michail Damaskinos was a monk here and worked in the monastery, and that the walls of his cell were covered with paintings.

We return to the main road. As we cross a verdant stream-bed shortly before entering the village of **Voriza**, we see the **Varsamonerou Monastery** to our left. This used to be an important foundation, with the Vrontisiou Monastery as one of its dependencies. Today it is ruined, and only the triple-aisled church of St Fanourios has survived intact. This church is of architectural interest; two of its aisles run in one direction while the third, built at a different time, intersects them at right angles. The wall-paintings in the church and its portable icons (many of which have been transferred to the St Catherine Monastery in Herakleio) are of considerable importance for the study of icon-painting in Crete.

We bypass Voriza and, at 53 km. from Herakleio, come to the pretty village of **Kamares**, which stands at an altitude of 600 m. It is a major centre for the production of folk art items and handicrafts. Above Kamares to the north west is the famous **Kamares Cave** where Minoan pottery dating back to 2000 BC was found; this pottery has become known as 'Kamares ware'. The pottery is in the Early Palace style, with a black background and bright red and white decoration. It has been concluded from the style of this pottery and the fact that it was found in the cave that the inhabitants of Phaistos used to leave offerings to the deity which was worshipped there.

The theatre at ancient Gortyn.

3. Ayii Deka, Gortyn, Phaestos, Matala

We leave the city Herakleio along the Messara road. At 29 km we come to the village of Ayia Varvara. After we leave the village, there is a good place to stop and admire the surrounding landscape. To the south, there is a fine view of the plain of Messara, the bread-basket of Crete, with its tiny white villages. To the east, the Lasithiotika mountains can be dimly discerned, and to the west the azure embrace of the Gulf of Messara can be seen. The road runs down to the village of Ayii Deka.

44 km. **Ayii Deka**. The village stands on a wooded hill and has a wonderful view over the ruins of ancient Gortyn across the olive groves of the northern end of the Messara plain. It is believed that its site was the cemetery of the ancient city. There is a small museum with finds from the area.

After 1 km. to west of Ayii Deka, we come to **Ancient Gortyn**, the archaeological site of which straddles the road to north and south. The ruins cover an enormous area. Gortyns is one of the most ancient cities on Crete and it dominated the Messara plain from pre-historic times into the Classical period.

The site was inhabited by the Minoans, but it did not develop into a city until after the Dorian invasion. Plato describes it as one of the richest cities of Crete. The law-abiding nature of the Gortynians is demonstrated by the large slabs bearing the city's laws which were built into the Odeum. This is the famous *Code* or *Law of Gortyn*, on whose principles many of the provisions of modern criminal law are still based. The text is in the Doric dialect and is writ-ten boustrophedon — that is, the first line is read from right to left and the next from left to right, as though one were ploughing a field. It dates from the late 6th or early 5th century BC. The provisions include rules of civil procedure and the fundamentals of civil, family, agrarian and commercial law. No barbarous punishments for offenders were laid down and

the death penalty was not pro-vided for; on the other hand, it was essential that the objec-tive guilt or innocence of the person charged be proved.

The Gortynians had friendly relations with the Achaeans and later with the Ptolemies of Egypt. They took the side of the Romans at a time when Knossos was opposed to the new power, with the ultimate aim of securing the domination of Crete. Thus Gortyn escaped the destruction by the Romans which was the fate of other Cretan cities. When the Romans joined Crete and Cyrenacia as an administrative unit, Gortyn became its capital and continued to be the chief city of Crete even in later times.

It was also the first city in Crete to feel the influence of Christianity and the first Chris-tian churches were built there. The oldest and most important of these buildings is the metropolitan basilica of *St Titus*, dating from the 6th cen-tury, the ruins of which can still be seen today.

The city continued to flourish until 828, when the Arabs took Crete and razed it.

Archaeological investigations have brought to light only a part of the ancient city. Among the most interesting features are the *acropolis*, on its hilltop, and the *concave theatre* below it. To the south of the Herakleio - Phaestos road lies the *Praetorium*, which was the seat of the Roman commander. To the west of this is the *Temple of Apollo Pythius,* dating from the 7th century. To the south of the temple is a *theatre* and to the north lies the *temple of Isis and Serapis*. Further south are the *amphitheatre, the baths* and the 2nd century *stadium.*

On the north side of the road are the ruins of the *Agora,* with a *temple of Asklepios* and the *Odeum* into whose rear wall the plaques with the laws were built.

53 km Mires, which has developed into a communications, commercial and agricultural town of major importance, and is the seat of the Bishop of Gortyn and Arkadia. The large park just outside the town is well worth a visit.

After we leave Mires, we continue west. To the right, at a short distance, we can seen among the trees which surround it the **Monastery of Our Lady 'Kalyviani'**. The little church had fallen into disrepair and was no longer used when in 1873 a wonder-working icon of Our Lady was found there; today it is housed in the modern church. The church we see today, work on which began in 1911 and was completed in 1924, is in the Byzantine style, with three aisles and a dome. In 1958, Bishop Timotheos (of Arkadia) began to use the revenues of the church to set up a number of foundations (a girl's orphanage, an old people's home, a school of domestic economy, etc.) which in 1961 were recognised as a monastic house. This new

Gortyn: the church of St Titus.

monastic complex is now the largest in Crete, with a reputation which stretches far beyond the island and attracts many thousands of pilgrims.

From here, the road runs on to village of **Tymbaki**. Today, the area's wonderful climate and the intensive cultivation of early vegetables in greenhouses have helped to turn Tymbaki into an important agricultural centre.

Close to Tymbaki to the west is **Kokkinos Pyrgos**, an ideal bathing beach on the Libyan Sea.

At 61 km. there is a turning to the left; a fine surfaced road leads us in 2 km. to the famous archaeological site of **Phaestos**.

The territory controlled by Phaestos ran from Cape Lithino to Psychio (Melissa) and included the Paximadia islets. Thus it dominated the plain of Messara and its ports were Kommos and

Matala. According to the myths, the dynasty which ruled Phaestos was founded by Rhadamanthus, son of Zeus, who was the brother of Minos and sat in judgement in the Underworld. During the Archaic, Classical and Hellenistic periods Phaestos retained its independence, but as a poor shadow of its status in Minoan times, when it was an important religious, administrative and economic centre. It participated in the Achaean campaign against Troy, sending troops along with the other Cretan cities.

Archaeological investigation of the site has revealed two successive phases of palace-building; the Early Palace period (1900-1700 BC), after which the buildings were destroyed by earthquake, and the New Palace period (1650-1400 BC). Most of the ruins which can be seen today are from the second of these periods. The archaeological site of Phaestos is the island's second most important, after Knossos. In some ways, it could be said that its palace is in better condition than that at Knossos, since the archaeologists working here used different principles and avoided reconstruction altogether. Many of the objects found on the site, which are of tremendous importance for our knowledge of Minoan civilisation, can be seen in Herakleio Archaeological Museum. Perhaps the most important is the so-called 'Phaestos Disc', which is held to be the oldest example of hieroglyphic writing ever found and is believed to record a hymn to the goddess Rhea.

The Minoan Palace of Phaestos stands on a hill 100 m high, with a panoramic view in all directions.

The excavations which brought this marvellous palace to life were conducted by Italian archaeologists, of whom the first was Federico Halbherr, in 1900. A brief tour of the palace will take at least two hours.

The Palaces

We start from the tourist pavilion at the upper end of the wall and enter the site by the *North West Entrance*. Here is the paved *North West Court*, where the foundations of buildings from Greek and Roman times can be seen over the remains of the Old Palace, which at Phaestos are much more numerous than at other sites. The Court is crossed by a raised *processional ramp*, which had also been part of the first palace. To the north east of the North West Court, a staircase leads to the larger, paved, *West Court*, which lies at a level six metres lower. On the north side of the Court are eight rows of seats, which

together with the Court itself form the *'theatral area'* for ceremonies and performances. When the New Palace was built, the whole West Court was raised, involving the covering over of four rows of seats in the theatre, and the new building went up seven metres to the east of the old one.

The processional way from the North West Court continues past the seats in the theatre and, in the middle of the West Court, forks: one branch leads west to the *deep pits* and ends on the south side. Here there was an imposing *Propylaeum* to a staircase which led to a corridor into the Central Court. To the south of this Propylaeum were the storerooms of the Old Palace, where multi-coloured Middle Minoan pottery came to light, together with the head of a clay statuette which gives a clear idea of the Minoan concept of the human form.

The Phaestos archaeological site.

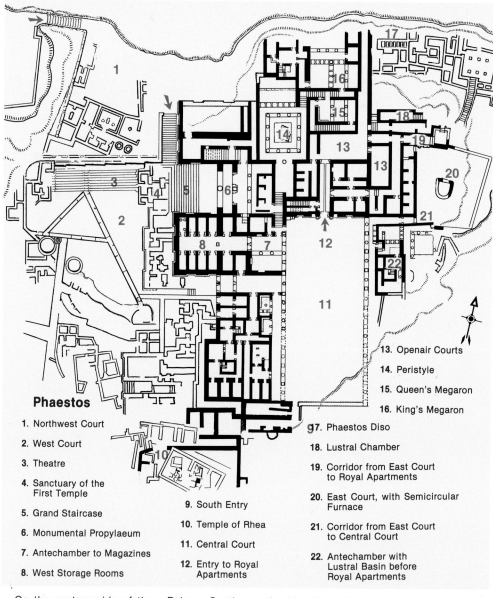

Phaestos

1. Northwest Court

2. West Court

3. Theatre

4. Sanctuary of the First Temple

5. Grand Staircase

6. Monumental Propylaeum

7. Antechamber to Magazines

8. West Storage Rooms

9. South Entry

10. Temple of Rhea

11. Central Court

12. Entry to Royal Apartments

13. Openair Courts

14. Peristyle

15. Queen's Megaron

16. King's Megaron

17. Phaestos Diso

18. Lustral Chamber

19. Corridor from East Court to Royal Apartments

20. East Court, with Semicircular Furnace

21. Corridor from East Court to Central Court

22. Antechamber with Lustral Basin before Royal Apartments

On the eastern side of the West Court, opposite the theatral area, is the *Great Staircase*, a marvellous example of Minoan architecture; its 12 steps are slightly convex so as to stop the rainwater from gathering in puddles on them. This staircase leads to the impressive *Propylaea* of the New Palace. Beneath here we can see the storerooms of the Old Palace. On the north side of the colonnade, another imposing staircase with large windows on the east and north sides of its landing led up to the royal apartments. Behind the colonnade to the east was a lightshaft with three columns, and next to it an openair courtyard. Another narrow staircase, to the south, led to the paved antechamber to the store-rooms, which, to the east, communicated with the Central Court, while a narrow corridor began on its western side. The store-rooms lay to the left and right of this corridor. In the last store-room to the north there are still jars which were used to preserve various products and which are decorated with horizontal bands in relief.

From the antechamber to the store-rooms we emerge into the paved *Central Court*. To the east and west of the Court, pillars and columns formed a colonnade to separate it from the various wings of the Palace. The south eastern side of the Court, where there may have been other apartments, has disappeared altogether. On the southwest side, where the *South Entrance* is, there are two rooms which may have been used as resting-quarters. On the eastern side of the Central Court there is a group of rooms.

On the north side of the Central Court, the pillars which can still be seen today testify to the existence of a colonnade. The two recesses to the right and left of the entrance were probably guard posts, for this was the entrance to the royal apartments. The imposing painted door in the colonnade led into a paved corridor which ended in two open-air courtyards, both of which belonged to the Old Palace. Along the first north western side, the Palace had three storeys. On the first was an antechamber. On the second floor, the staircase brings us out at the famous *Peristyle Hall*, a square room with four columns along each side, which communicates via six doors with another spacious loggia-like hall. This was probably the *Queen's Megaron;* it had a floor paved with alabaster, benches and a light shaft. To the north is the *King's Megaron*, whose walls were decorated with paintings. The western extremity of this complex of rooms contains an elegant lustral basin — or perhaps it was a bath-tub. To the north east extends the complex of buildings comprising the Old Palace. In one of its halls, brick partitions create seven smaller rooms, and it is believed that this was the *Archive*. **In one of the rooms, the**

famous Phaestos Disk was found; although its hieroglyphic script has not been deciphered even today, we can admire it in the Herakleio Archaeological Museum. The disk bears symbols on both sides, written from the outside towards the centre in spiral fashion. The characters were stamped on the disk using moulds and that is why the disk is sometimes described as the oldest piece of printing to have survived. The text is believed to be a hymn to the goddess Rhea.

In the last hall to the east in this complex of buildings, archaeologists discovered a large number of unused pots arranged in rows, which suggests that it was a pottery workshop. To the east of the workshop there are remains of the paved road which led down into the plain to the east of the Palace.

To the west of Phaestos, at a distance of 3 km. are the remains of the royal palace of **Ayia Triada**. In Minoan times, a paved road ran directly from Ayia Triada to Phaestos, and traces of it can still be seen, with its asymmetrical stone slabs.

The royal palace of Ayia Triada may have been the summer residence of the kings of Phaestos. The hill on which it stands was inhabited as far back as the Stone Age, but the palace itself dates from about

1600 BC, when Phaestos and Knossos were at the height of their prosperity. The floor-plan of the palace is simpler than that of the other Minoan buildings, and is L-shaped. The characteristic central court is missing, as are the lustral water-tanks. However, the palace must have been luxurious and continues to be imposing. Historically, it had the same fate as Phaestos and Knossos, being destroyed around 1400 BC. At some later date, another grand building, rectangular in shape and with a colonnade, was erected on the site. By the Geometrical period the palace was no longer inhabited, but it continued to be a place of worship, as can be seen from the clay statuettes which have been found there. In the Hellenistic period, a small sanctuary to Zeus occupied the site.

Close at hand, on the spot known as 'Kamilari', a Middle Minoan tomb has come to light. In one of the tombs, the famous stone Sacrophagus of Ayia Triada was found; decorated with religious and cult scenes, it can be seen in Herakleio Archaeological Museum today. The same museum also contains many other finds from Ayia Triada.

We return to the Phaestos -Matala road and turn south west. We travel across the fertile plain, whose verdure is most restful to the eye. We soon come to the pretty village of **Pitsidia**, to the west of which, by the shore, is the archaeological site of **Kommos**. This was an ancient settlement, the first harbour which Phaestos possessed, and it has been revealed by archaeological investigations. The settlement is believed to date from the late Bronze Age. According to the myths, Kommos was where King Menelaus of Sparta's ships sank as he sailed home from Troy.

The road ends on the western coast of the Eparchy of Pyrgiotissa, at **Matala**. Matala is the natural outlet of Phaestos on the sea, and in the Minoan period it was the palace's second harbour. After the destruction of Phaestos in 220 BC, its ownership passed to Gortyn.

There is a semi-circular sandy beach 300 metres in length, at either end of which are the cliffs which make the cove a rather private place. These cliffs are riddled with man-made caves hacked out of the rock. Once the famous caves of Matala were the homes of the fisherfolk who lived here, but during the 1970s they became one of the centres of the international hippy movement. Today, the caves have been fenced off by the Archaeological Service and it is forbidden to stay or spend the night in them.

Tombs from Greek, Roman and Early Christian times have been found in the caves, and it is believed that they were first inhabited —by the living— in the pre-historic period. There are also underwater caves, which can be visited by boat. Shipwrecks have been identified on the sea-bed, and archaeological finds, particularly from Roman times, are very common in the area.

Matala has a fine, mild climate, and this, together with its fine beach and sheltered bay, have made it an ideal place for bathing even in the winter months. In the summer, there is a daily caique service from Matala to Ayia Galini in the Prefecture of Rethymno.

Caves in the rock, a sandy beach running to a pretty cove and a mild climate - the features which made Matala famous.

4. Lendas, Kali Limenes

We leave Herakleio via the Messara road as far as Ayii Deka, 44 km away. After the Gortyn archaeological site, we turn left and at 46 km we get our first sight of the attractive village of **Mitropoli**. The village takes its name (which means 'bishopric') from the fact that the first bishop's see in Crete was established here in early Byzantine times. The village stands almost on top of the remains of ancient Gortyn. Recently, an Early Christian basilica with richly-coloured mosaic floors was discovered here.

At 51 km we reach **Platanos**, where General Katehakis was born. The vicinity of the village has yielded two of the largest Early Minoan tombs ever to be found.

At 53 km we come to **Plora**, identified with ancient Pyloros. A Roman marble bust of Dionysus was found nearby.

Now the road begins to run downhill, towards the sea. The little fishing village of **Lendas** lies on the south coast of Crete, on a promontory in the shape of a crouching lion which runs down to a white strip of fine sand 300 metres in length before merging into the azure of the Libyan Sea. According to the myths, one of the lions which pulled the goddess Rhea's chariot was turned into stone here, thus giving the area its name.

Today, Lendas is an ideal holiday resort, which attracts large numbers of visitors drawn by the natural beauties of the spot and by its medicinal spring, whose waters are reputed to be efficacious in the treatment of disorders of the stomach and the blood. The spring was known in ancient times, and because of it there was a sanctuary to Asklepios, the god of healing. Ancient **Leben** was the port for Gortyn, and it had trading links with Egypt. In Classical and Roman times, when it was at the peak of its prosperity, it was a sacred city. The divinities of Asklepios and Hygeia were worshipped here, and the Askleipeion, or sanctuary of Asklepios, attracted visitors from all over Crete and from Libya as well. The *Treasury* is the oldest of all the monuments which have survived on the site. This is a square well, constisting of seven rows of ashlar masonry. The famous Asklepeio had a fine temple with a superb mosaic; the altar to the god stood in the inner-

Lentas lies in the blue embrace of the Libyan Sea.

most recesses of the temple. There was an imposing marble staircase, colonnades on the eastern and western sides, and a sanctuary of the nymphs. The most important part of the Asklepeio was the Abaton or Adyton, which could be entered only by the priests and the pilgrims who came to the sanctuary as patients; after their sojourn in the Abaton they emerged cured. There was accommodation for the priests and for the pilgrims. In addition, there were lustral facilities for the patients, and it was at this time that the medicinal spring came to light.

From here we can visit the **Hodeghetria** and **Apezanon monasteries, or our route can be continued by car or caique to Kali Limenes.**

77 km. Kali Limenes. There is an outstanding beach, two kilometres in length, whose white sand provides a superb contrast with the blue of the water. The pretty little village with its harbour is ample compasation for the time and trouble it may take to reach this remote corner of southern Crete. Opposite the modern village are the islets known as **Megalo** and **Mikro.** The climate is warm even in winter — so warm that in this part of the island the tortoises do not hibernate. Indeed, the very name of the place says something of its nature, for this is the 'Fair Havens' of St Paul.

St Paul landed here when on his way to Rome; this was where the teaching of Christianity in Crete began, and here St Titus was ordained as the first bishop of Crete. The port for Gortyn was here in Roman times, when the area flourished. The town was independent and there were temples to Asklepios and the goddess Isis. Today there are installations for supplying ocean-going vessels.

5. Archanes, Vathypetro, Apanosifi Monastery

From the city of Herakleio (Eleftherias Square) we exit through the New Gate ('Kainourgia Porta'). We take the good surfaced road for Knossos, which we pass on our left 5 km. out of the town. The landscape is peaceful, and the green of vineyards and olive groves is the dominant colour. A turning to the left leads to Skalani, Varvari and the Kazantzakis Museum. After 10 km. a turning to the right leads in 6 km. to the little town of **Archanes**, which stands on the slopes of a low hill; the surrounding countryside contains numerous vineyards and there are streams everywhere. This area produces the best Cretan table grapes (known as 'rozakia') and the famous Archanes wine is made. The little town of Archanes consists of picturesque narrow lanes and neo-Classical houses whose balconies and courtyards are like a permanent floral exhibition.

Nearby, traces have been found of a Minoan house which dates from approximately 1450 BC - that is, from about the time at which the last buildings in Knossos were erected. To the north west of Archanes, at the spot known as **Fourni**, archaeological investigations in the late 1960s brought to light the largest necropolis ever found in Crete. It consists of tholos tombs with chambers hewn out of the rock, as well as groups of shaft graves. The cemetery was used between the Early Minoan and Minoan periods.

At Anemospilia, 3.5 km. from Archanes on the north western slopes of Mt Yiouchtas, the only known Minoan temple was found. The temple, which was destroyed by an earthquake in about 1700 BC, contained an altar and there is evidence that human sacrifice was carried out there - perhaps in an effort to appease the gods and stave off the impending catastrophe.

The Venetian period, too, has left its mark on this area. There are also two Byzantine churches, that of the Holy Trinity and that of St Paraskevi, which have fine wall-paintings.

Archanes stands on a site which faces the sacred mountain of Yiouchtas. According to the myths, the summit of Yiouchtas was the spot where Zeus chose to die.

From Archanes we turn south and, after 3 km., reach **Vathypetro**, a small settlement which is uninhabited today. At the spot known as Piso Livadia, on a fine site with a good view of the valley and slightly off the road, is a Minoan house. This was in fact a farmhouse, the only one of its type discovered to date, as demonstrated by the looms, pottery workshop, olive press and grape press (for wine) found inside it. It will be remembered that even today the best varieties of grape come from around here.

Afther Vathypetro, the road leads (23 km) to **Houdetsi** at an altitude of 440 m. About 5 km. further on, a turning to the right leads up to a pretty hill on which, amid the plane-tress and the gurgling of streams, is the **Monastery of St George 'Apanosifis'.** This is one of Crete's most important monasteries, and it also owns large areas of land. It was built about the year 1600 by the monk Paisios, with the help of the local lord, whose name was Longovardos. The monastery became very rich and, by providing shelter for freedom fighters, played an important part in the island's struggle for self-determination. It was also a major centre of learning where numerous Cretan priests were trained.

6. Kastelli, Viannos, Arvi

From Herakleio, we take the Knossos road, turning left after the archeological site and coming to the attractive village of **Skalani**, which has a fine view. The village is entered along a cobbled road with steps, which accounts for its name (from 'skala', a step).

22 km. Ayies Paraskeves is a most attractive village. It stands on a hilltop and has a panoramic view over the verdant plain of Peza. The top of the hill is dominated by the old church of St George, while the church of the Holy Girdle (Ayia Zoni), with wall-paintings, stands in the main square of the village.

After Ayies Paraskies a turning to the left leads to the pretty village of **Varvari**, recently renamed **Myrtia**, birthplace of the father of Nikos Kazantzakis. In the square of the village, a restored house serves as the **Nikos Kazantzakis Museum**, with a collection of personal effects, manuscripts, first editions and photographs of Crete's most important writer.

30 km. Thrapsano. Before Kastelli, a turning left leads, to Thrapsano. This village is a major centre for the making of pottery and it is worth visiting to see (and perhaps purchase something from) the workshops which supply the whole of Crete.

36 km. Kastelli, chief town of the Pediada Eparchy. The town stands on the eastern edge of a small plain known by the same name, a fertile area densely planted with vines and olives. On the site of the secondary school was a Venetian castle which was also called Kastelli. Near the entrance to the village a Roman cemetery has been discovered. This is a pretty and lively village, and it acts as the commercial and administrative centre for the whole surrounding area.

Six kilometres to the east of Kastelli, near the village of **Xidas**, are the remains of the ancient city of **Lyttos** or **Lyctos**. This city occupied a semicircular site on the foothills of the sacred mountain Dikti —which gave it its alternative name of Diktaia— in a high and easily fortified position. It was one of the oldest and most important cities of Doric Crete and for a time rivalled Knossos. Its exits to the sea were at Chersonisos and Milatos, on the northern shore of the bay of Mallia. As a Doric colony, it took part in the Trojan War. In its heyday, which occurred in historical times, it dominated the whole of eastern Crete. It was often at war with Knossos, which eventually destroyed it in 219 BC. It was rebuilt at a later date, but never regained its former glory. In the Roman period, Lyttos flourished once again. Various types of coin minted by it have been found, as well as coins from the Roman period.

Eight kilometres from Kastelli, a turning right takes us to **Arkalochori**, which is 33 km. from Herakleio. This is an important commercial and administrative centre.

We continue to run downhill and, at 43 km. pass the village of **Panayia**. At 63 km. we come to **Kato Viannos**.

65 km. Ano Viannos, built in a semicircle on the slope forming the foothills' of Mt Dikti, has a fine view over the most fertile olive groves in the Viannos Eparchy, of which it is the chief town. The modern settlement stands on the site of the ancient city of Biannos, which was independent and issued its own coins, showing the head of a woman on one side and a flower on the other. In Venetian times Viannos was a large and prosperous village, but under the Turks it was destroyed twice, in 1822 and in 1866. Today, it is a

verdant settlement with numerous streams of fresh water and a mild climate. Steep and narrow lanes lined with houses in the traditional architectural style lead up to pretty little squares with stone-built fountains from which cool water flows. The site of the village is dominated by plane trees, birches and myrtles, and the little cafés under the shade of their branches add another cooling note. The village is known for its olive-oil, its carobs and its dairy products.

It is also an important communications junction, as it stands on the Herakleio -Ierapetra road and is the starting-point for access to the sandy beaches of **Arvi, Psari Forada, Keratokambos** and **Tsoutsouro** on the Libyan Sea.

Viannos was the birthplace of Yannis Kondylakis, one of the most important modern Greek prose writers and journalists.

Among other sights in the village is the church of St Pelagia, with wall-paintings of 1360.

We leave Ano Viannos and head east. After 6 km. we come to the village of **Amira**. Here we fork south and cross a plain with banana trees before running downhill to the beautiful beach of the village of **Arvi**. The white sandy beach and the almost tropical climate make this an ideal bathing-place, even in the winter. The imposing gorge known as Axio Theas is nearby, while the yellow and green of the banana plantations are the dominant colours. To the east of the gorge is a monastery of St Anthony. The village preserves the name of the Helleno-Roman settlement on the same site.

We return to Amira, where the eastern fork in the road passes through the village of **Pefko** before crossing into the Prefecture of Lasithi and eventually leading to Ierapetra after Myrto, on the coast.

7. Tylisos, Fodele, Ayia Pelagia

We leave the city of Herakleio along the old 'national road' for Chania. The road is surfaced but winding. After 6 km. we come to the village of **Gazi**, on the banks of the river Galanos. We continue and at about 10 km come to the traditional village of **Arolithos**, set among gorse and broom. In the village. It strikes the visitor that life is as it was a hundred or more years ago. Yet the village is a modern one, built on the initiative of private enterprise. Its houses and other buildings

were constructed using the traditional methods; that, in a way, has given it its name, since 'arolithos' means a depression in the ground where rain-water gathers, and in the same manner the traditions of daily life and crafts have been preserved here.

From Arolithos, a turning to the left (south) makes its way across the small but very fertile plain of Tylisos; the main crops are vines and olives. At 13 km. across the verdant plain on the slopes of Mt Ida, we see **Tylisos**, which stands on the site of a Minoan city of the same name.

Archaeologists have discovered three Minoan houses here, dating from 1550-1450 BC —that is, from the same period as the second palaces at Knossos and Mallia. The archaeological site is next to a little pine wood to the east of the village.

We return to the junction at the tenth kilometre of the old 'national road' and head north west. Now we begin to climb, with an excellent view of the city of Herakleio to the east. At 20 km. we pass the attractive village **Marathos**. At km. 21, a turning to the right leads to the historic **St Pantaleimon Monastery** and to the picturesque village of **Fodele**.

After a run of approximately 7 km. through a densely-vegetated valley, we see Fodele among its lemon and orange trees and under its plane-trees. Through the village runs the Pantomoundrios river, known simply as 'the river' to the locals. It flows into the sea at a sandy beachy in a pretty cove; this beach, like many on the north coast of Crete, is exposed to the etesian winds of summer (the meltemi), which make it a good place for wind-surfing.

The attractive resort of Ayia Pelagia, sheltered from the north winds of the Cretan Sea.

The archaeologists identify the bay at Fodele with ancient Astale, the port for Axos. Others say that Fodele itself was the ancient city of Pantomatrion. According to one version of the story, Fodele was the birthplace, in 1545, of the famous painter Domenico Theotokopoulos (El Greco), who lived and made his name at Toledo in Spain. His art was considerably influenced by the Cretan school of icon-painting. There is a bust of El Greco in the village square, while at the spot known as Skoteini a group of ruined buildings is believed to have been his family's house. At the same location is an important cruciform church of the Presentation of Our Lady, dating from Late Byzantine times.

From Fodele, we take the new 'national road' for a while, in an easterly direction. After some eight kilometres we turn off this road and head down to the left, towards the coastal village of **Ayia Pelagia**, a modern tourist village which stretches along the shores of an attractive sheltered bay where the northerly winds of summer do not penetrate. A long beach with enticing yellow sand —which becomes coarser and white in some places— and little white pebbles accounts for the area's importance as a resort. Agia Pelagia and the little cove of **Lygaria** which lies about one kilometre away constitute a most attractive unit.

Ayia Pelagia takes its name from the church of St Pelagia which stood about 1 km. to the west of the bay and was a dependency of the Savvathianon Convent. On the northern shore of the bay is a cave known as 'Evresi' ('finding-place'), and it is said that an icon of the saint was discovered there.

This, according to the archaeologists, was the site of ancient Apollonia. At the spot known as Kladotos, recent digs have yielded both Minoan and Hellenistic finds. Chamber tombs of the Late Minoan period, hewn out of the rock, have also come to light. However, the main find was the Prytaneion, headquarters of the elders of the town, which was built in the 4th century BC and destroyed in the 2nd century. Houses have also been disovered, together with a pottery workshop.

We return to the crossroads. To the left, is the coastal village of **Linoperamata**. We take the old national road to the right, and after passing through the seaside tourist resort of **Ammoudara**, reach Herakleio.

The long beach of Ammoudara.

Amnisos: detail of the Lily frescoes.

The beach Kokkini Chani and Kato Gouves.

8. Amnisos, Chersonisos, Mallia

At 3 km. from the centre of town we come to the coastal suburb of **Nea Alikarnassos**, which was founded in 1925 by refugees from the town by the same name (ancient Halicarnassus) in Asia Minor. This is the site of Herakleio International Airport. We continue across the fertile plain of Karteros, which was once known as the Omphalio plain. At 7 km. we come to the beautiful beach of **Karteros**, while on our right are the ruins of ancient **Amnisos**, which surround the hill known today as **Palaiochora**.

Amnisos was the port of Knossos and Minos was said to have his shipyard at the Karteros river. It was at Amnisos, according to the myths, the Theseus disembarked when

he came to Crete to slay the Minotaur, and it was from here that Idomeneus, grandson of Minos, set out with 80 ships to help Agamemnon in the campaign against Troy. Odysseus, too, called here when wandering the Mediterranean on his tortuous way home to Ithaca. Archaeological investigations have revealed a Middle Minoan III villa with wonderful wall-paintings, including the lily frescoes to be seen in Herakleio Museum.

In 846, the Byzantine General Karteros landed at Amnisos to fight the Saracens, and in the end gave his name to the whole area.

From the top of the hill there is a wonderful view of the long beach with the white-topped waves of the Cretan Sea which sweep it, while in the distance we can see the islet of **Dias**. According to the myth, this islet

(whose name is the modern Greek form of 'Zeus') was the first place that Zeus reached after kidnapping Europa, princess of Sidon in Phoenicia (Lebanon, today), who became the mother of Minos, subsequently king of Knossos. In order to honour Europa, the whole continent was given her name. Today, the islet is uninhabited, and its sole use is as a habitat for the Cretan wild goat. Underwater investigations by Jacques Cousteau have revealed traces of a Minoan settlement.

On the slopes of the hill, above the road and next to a modern quarry, is the famous **Eileithyia Cave** or cave of the fairies. This was one of the earliest centres of worship on Crete, and it was dedicated to Eileithyia, daughter of Hera and protector of women in childbirth. The cave is very beautiful, with stalactities, pillars of rock and little lakes.

We return to the main road, still heading east. We cross the fertile Vatheianos plain, with its large area of fields. At 13 km. from Herakleio we come to the excellent beach of **Kokkino Chani**, which has fine white sand. The whole of this area is subject to strong north westerly winds and is good for windsurfing. To our right is the archaeological site of **Niros**. Excavations here have revealed a well-preserved Minoan building dating from about the time of the second palaces of Knossos and Phaistos.

At 15 km. we pass the attractive beach of **Gournes**. We continue, and at 20 km. come to the sandy beach of **Kato Gouves** or **Finikas**. A side-road to the right leads to the village of **Gouves**. After the village, a further side-road to the right takes us to the **Skoteinou Cave**. This natural feature is well worth a visit. It was one of the most important religious centres on Crete.

The harbour at Chersonisos: an organised tourist resort with abundant night-life.

At 23 km. there is a turning to the right which leads up to the Lasithi plateau. This is the road which will be taken by those whose trip began in western Crete and who wish to visit the plateau; it is the classic itinerary. Now we head east, and at 26 km. arrive at **Limani Chersonisou**, which stands on the western edge of the Bay of Mallia. It takes its name from the peninsula ('chersonisos') on which it stands and which creates two sheltered little bays with fine sandy beaches. Today, the village has developed into a well-organised tourist resort with all the necessary installations and a lively night-life. To the south of the harbour, not far away, is the village of **Chersonisos** in a verdant setting. The village remains the picturesque traditional settlement it has always

been, indifferent to the hum and bustle of the harbour.

To the west of the village stood the ancient city of Chersonesos, which was the port of ancient Lyttos. It was inhabited in prehistoric times, as can be seen from the traces of a Minoan settlement; it was autonomous, and minted its own coins, which showed the head of Artemis on one side and Apollo with a lyre on the other. It is believed that the first settlers were refugees from tyranny who brought with them the cult statue of Britomartis, 'the sweet virgin', a Minoan deity who was one of the most important figures in the Minoan pantheon. Later she became identified with Artemis. At the famous shrine in Chersonisos, Britomartis was worshipped because of her success in evading the

clutches of Minos. After he had laid siege to her for nine months, she threw herself into the sea to the east of Herakleio. The shrine, which has not survived, was Minoan, while the scanty remains to be seen today date from Roman times. There are the ruins of an acropolis, an amphitheatre and a theatre, an old harbour and a fountain with mosaics showing fishermen. The foundations of two Early Christian basilicas have also come to light, with mosaic floors whose tesserae are arranged in geometric shapes.

In the bay of Chersonisos there is an isolated rock whose shape is reminiscent of a female body upright out of the sea and holding a basin on its head. The locals call the rock 'the girl', and if asked have numerous tales to tell about it.

The road continues along the coast, to the pretty cove of **Stalida**, 32 km. from Herakleio. This is an attractive tourist resort with abundant greenery and market gardens. There is an excellent beach with fine, white sand.

From Stalida, a side-road to the right climbs up through dense olive groves to **Mochos**. This village stands at an altitude of 400 metres and has a panoramic view over Mallia Bay. Picturesque alleys lead to fine houses with courtyards crammed with flowers, and in the centre of the village there is a large square with a dance floor. On 15 August each year, the Herakleio Travel Club organises a festival of folk dance and song.

From Mochos the road continues upwards to the Lasithi plateau.

The other side of Chersonisos.

The pretty bay of Stalida has a fine beach and dense vegetation.

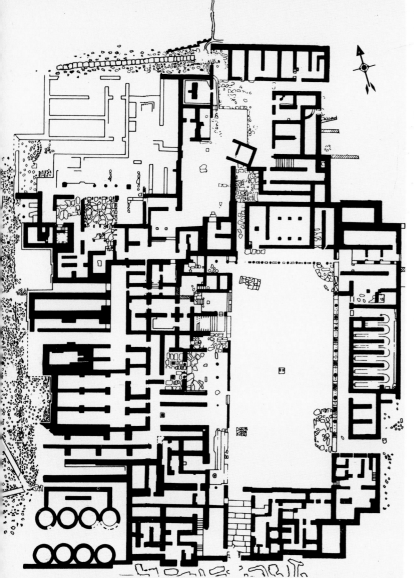

Mallia

1. West Court
2. Eight Circular Granaries
3. West Storage Rooms
4. Portico
5. Magazines
6. Weapons Room, where the royal sceptre was found
7. Loggia
8. Grand Staircase
9. South Entry
10. Kernos (Circular Stone for Offerings)
11. Broad Staircase
12. Southeast Entry
13. East Storage Rooms
14. Central Court
15. Hall Pillars
16. North Court
17. North Storage Rooms
18. Northeast Entry
19. North Entry
20. Olive Press
21. Palace Court

34 km. Mallia is a modern town, in a fertile area well supplied with water and noted for its market produce and windmills. It has its own beach, with fine, white sand; one of Crete's finest. The pretty old village lies to the west of the main road, guarding its traditions; tourism has hardly touched it. The archaeological site lies approximately 3 km. to the east of the town.

This was the site of an important Minoan town whose ancient name is unknown to us. The contemporary name comes from the word 'omalia' ('flat'), thus indicating the lie of the terrain. Under the Venetians and the Turks, Mallia was an important place. Archaeological finds have shown that the ancient city prospered between the Early and Late Minoan periods. Here the ruling dynasty was that of Sarpedon, brother of Minos and Rhadamanthus. The city issued its own coinage, which had a head of Athena on one side and two dolphins on the other. At the spot known as Chrysolakkos, a Minoan cemetery has been found and yielded gold funeral offerings. *Among them was the fine piece of jewellery with two bees which can be seen today in Herakleio Museum.* But the most important discovery of all was the city palace, which occupied an area of 8,000 square metres and dates from the same time as the palace of

Knossos. It is also laid out to the same plan as Knossos. One of the four largest Minoan palaces found so far, it is situated in a valley, at some distance from the sea. Although it does not possess the majesty of Knossos or Phaestos, and has neither their wall-paintings nor their theatres, it is nonetheless imposing and fascinating. Like all the other Minoan palaces, it was destroyed by earthquake around 1700 BC and later rebuilt in the form we see today. It, too, has a long and narrow central court, surrounded by four wings with five entrances. The western side of the palace is the most important and impressive.

From Mallia the road continues to the south east into the hinterland, and after passing through the impressive gorge of Ayios Yeorgios 'Selinaris' arrives at Ayios Nikolaos.

Mallia. Above: The Archaeological site, below: the beach.

THE PREFECTURE OF LASITHI:
The Prefecture of Lasithi occupies the esternmost part of Crete and has an area of 1,818 square kilometres. Its population totals approximately 70,000 and the principal occupations are farming and stock-breading. The main products of the Prefecture are cereals, olive oil, olives, carobs and currants. Thanks to the warm —almost African— climate of the southern provinces of the Prefecture, there is considerable production of early vegetables and bananas. The Ierapetra and Gra Lygia areas, in particular, which have the highest number of hours of sunshine and the lowest rainfall, have developed into important centres for the production of early vegetables, and especially tomatoes. The Lasithi plateau is among the most fertile parts of the province; it produces large quantities of potatoes and very high-quality apples. The windmills —there are more than 10,000 of them— which visitors today can see scattered across the plateau are used to irrigate the soil. On the Lasithi Plateau is the fine Diktaean Cave, where according to the myths Zeus was born. In this area, the spades of archaeologists have brought abundant finds to light.

There are two theories as to the origin of the name 'lasithi': the first relates it to the ancient Greek word 'lasios', which means fertile area —and indeed Lasithi has been verdant since ancient times—

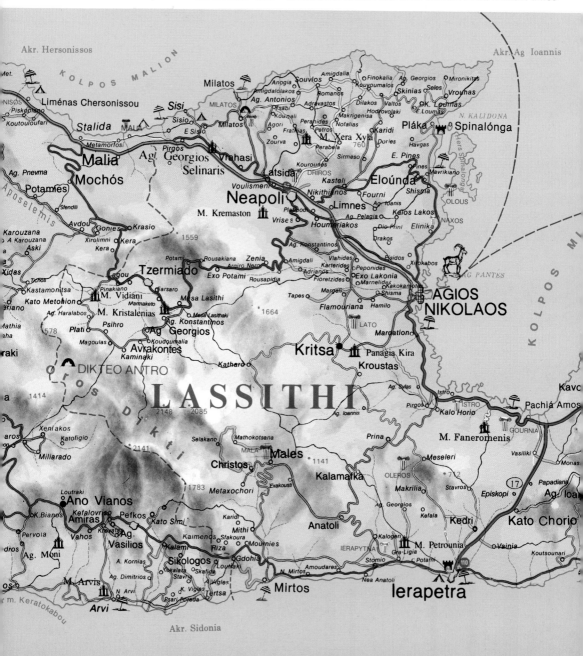

while the second, attributed to Paul Favre, relates the name to Siteia, which the Venetians rendered 'La Sitti'. The capital of the Prefecture is Ayios Nikolaos, an attractive little harbour standing on a deep bay. Ayios Nikolaos and nearby Elounda have developed into tourist resorts of major importance, with many large hotel complexes. However, quiet beaches, isolated cafes and striking interchanges of landscape can still be found throughout the Prefecture — the famous palm forest at Vai, for example, or the forest of pines and wild cypresses at Selekano. There are important archaeological and historical sites, too, such as the palace of Zakros, and the admirable monastery of Toplou, with its long history and links with the Patriarchate.

Communications by sea between the Prefecture and Piraeus are conducted through Herakleio. There are also sailings for Piraeus from Ayios Nikolaos and Siteia, via the Cyclades. Buses meet the flights into Herakleio airport. Siteia airport has flights for Rhodes, Carpathos and Kasos. Caiques and tourist craft sail to the islets of Spinalonga and Chrysi. Inside the Prefecture itself, the villages are served by the town and long-distance KTEL buses.

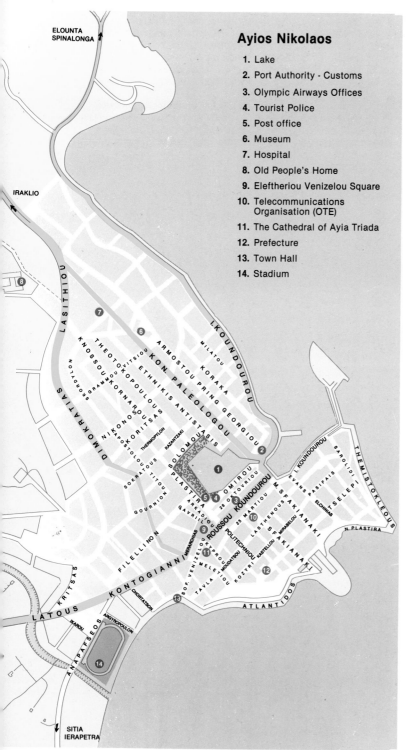

Ayios Nikolaos

1. Lake
2. Port Authority - Customs
3. Olympic Airways Offices
4. Tourist Police
5. Post office
6. Museum
7. Hospital
8. Old People's Home
9. Eleftheriou Venizelou Square
10. Telecommunications Organisation (OTE)
11. The Cathedral of Ayia Triada
12. Prefecture
13. Town Hall
14. Stadium

The town of Ayios Nikolaos

Ayios Nikolaos is the capital of the Prefecture of Lasithi and, according to the 1981 census, has a population of 8,130. Protected by mountains, the town stands on a little promontory on the western side of the peaceful Bay of Mirabello. Thanks to its warm climate and its calm sea it has developed into a leading resort centre, with large hotels, and it has expanded quite considerably. Its harbour, whose moorings are sheltered from the wind, is the base for countless pleasure craft and fishing-boats.

No other town in Crete can rival the tourist trade of Ayios Nikolaos. During the summer months, the harbour area, with its numerous restaurants, cafés and patisseries, hums with life and the atmosphere is cosmopolitan.

Despite this, the town has managed to retain much of the picturesqueness of the past, particularly in the centre, which has houses built in the traditional architectural style, narrow alleyways and cobbled steps. From the harbour, a seaside avenue leads (right) to a cobbled square with fish tavernas at the water's edge.

Another attraction is the little round lake by the harbour known as Voulismeni or Vromolimni, where according to the myths the goddess Athena came to wash. The lake must have been created by subsidence through volcanic action; it is nowhere wider than 137 metres and its depth is up to 67 metres. Today, a canal in which the fishing-boats anchor links it to the sea.

Ayios Nikolaos: the town, the harbour and the circular Voulismeni lake.

In antiquity, there was a small harbour called Lato towards Kamara at this point; it was the outlet to the sea of the Doric city of Lato or Etera, which stood on the spot called Goulas today. In the 3rd century BC the harbour was of considerable economic importance and minted its own coins.

In the 13th century, the Bay of Mirabello took its name from the fortress erected there by the Genoese. Not a trace has remained of the castle, which stood on a rise to the west of the harbour.

The town was given its current name in the 16th century, by the Venetians; the little chapel of St Nicholas from which the name comes can still be seen today, on the pro-montary opposite the Minos Palace hotel. The chapel, a single-aisled structure with a dome, is very old and has wall-paintings in two layers; they are among the finest on Crete. The first layer is post-Iconoclastic (9th century) and has geometrical and natural motifs. The town began to develop after 1870, when many refugees from Sfakia settled there to escape the bloody fighting which for decades had been the order of the day in their home town. But it was not until tourism came that Ayios Nikolaos acquired a world-wide reputation.

The **Archaeological Museum** of Ayios Nikolaos was founded in 1970 and is housed in a modern building. Its collection consists of recent finds from eastern Crete. In the ante-chamber there is Minoan pottery from a shipwreck in Mirabello Bay. Gallery I has statuettes and pottery dating from 3000-2300 BC. Gallery II (case 16) has a libation vessel in human form, from Myrtos. This is an Early Minoan masterpiece. The finds from a child's tomb are also on show. Gallery Ω contains 7th century BC terracotta figurines, while the next gallery, marked ΩI, contains finds from Olounda. Gallery ΩII has finds from Roman tombs; note in particular a skull with a golden crown.

The town also has the Koundoureios Municipal Library, with a collection of 10,000 volumes.

To the north of the harbour
of Ayios Nikolaos are beaches
of pebbles and rocks. Sandy
beaches can be found on the
northern edge of the town, at
the cove of **Ammoudi**, at **Hava-
nia** and at **Ammoudara**. To the
south of the town, at Istros, is
the beautiful **Bay of Voulisma**
with its blue-green waters and
yellow sandy beach.

Trips from Ayios Nikolaos

1. Elounda, Spinalonga, Plaka.
2. Neapoli, Lasithi Plateau.
3. Kritsa, Lato Hetera.
4. Mochlos, Siteia.
5. Toplou Monastery, Vai.
6. Palaikastro, Kato Zakros.
7. Episkopi, Praissos.
8. Pacheia Ammos, Ierapetra.

Our acquaintance with e-
stern Crete starts from our base at Ayios Nikolaos.

Pleasure craft waiting at the sheltered quay.

There are fine beaches to the north of the harbour.

Elounda: a world-famous tourist resort with modern amenities.

1. Spinalonga, Elounda, Plaka

Spinalonga peninsula: This lies opposite Elound and is joined to its eastern shore, forming a sheltered bay. Today, the peninsula is joined to the main body of the island by an isthmus cut by French sailors in the late 19th century and known as Poros. A narrow bridge crosses from the island to Spinalonga, next to a windmill which has been converted into a picturesque café.

This was the site of ancient Olous, near to the city of Naxos, the whole of which sank into the sea, as proved by the ruins which can be seen on the seabed when the weather is calm. It was an independent and autonomous city.

To the east of this area, near the isthmus and next to the little white chapel which can be seen today, are the ruins of a basilica; it has a mosaic floor in-corporating designs with fish and plants.

To the south of Elounda are the remains of a rectangular building of the Geometric period. From the finds made on the site, the archaeologists have concluded that this must have been a temple to the immortal lovers, Aphrodite and Ares.

Elounda today consists of seven different sections, of which **Schisma**, by the sea, is the most lively in the summer. The whole area is an enormous tourist resort, with the most modern facilities, and it attracts visitors from all over the world.

From Elounda there are boat-trips to the rocky islet of **Spinalonga**. The islet, which in 1954 was renamed **Kalydonia**, lies off the northern tip of the peninsula. In 1579, the Venetians built a seemingly impregnable castle on the rock of Spinalonga, whose dimensions are only 200 × 400 m. The castle was designed to protect Elounda Bay and the whole of Mirabello as well. Throughout the Turkish-Venetian war, which lasted 24 whole years, the castle, with its enormous cannon, resisted every attempt to capture it. And when the Turks finally took the rest of Crete, in 1699, Spinalonga remained in Venetian hands along with Gramvousa and Suda in western Crete. It was not until 1715, by a special treaty between the two warring states, that it passed into Turkish hands.

We enter the fortress between two strong battlements and beneath the Moncenigo battlement, on which most of the cannon were placed. The main line of defence, with double battlements, faced east. After the rise in the ground was a further line of defence. The San Michele bastion protected the northern shore, while the rest of the castle buildings were on the western side, which was safe from attack.

The name Spinalonga is a corruption of the Greek phrase 'stin Elounda', 'at Elounda'; from this corruption, the Venetians and Greeks managed to produce the name Macracantha: spina = acantha (thorn) and longa = makra (long). However, whatever name was used later came to be synonymous with human misery, for in 1903 the castle was turned into a leper colony. Fortunately, the advances of science enabled the colony to be closed in 1957.

From Elounda we continue north, and having passed the pretty spot of **Tsifliki Eloundas** at 12 km, we come to **Plaka** (15 km.). This is an attractive fishing village with a picturesque harbour and a beach with fine white pebbles and clear blue water.

The rocky islet of Spinalonga, with its impregnable Venetian fortress.

Elounda bay

2. Neapoli, Lasithi Plateau

15 km. Neapoli: In the middle of the fertile and verdant plain of Mirabello, there is one of the most handsome and important towns on the island. Today, Neapoli is an attractive commercial centre, laid out on a rational town plan. It has fine modern buildings and the installations of a School of Domestic Science.

Milatos lies 11 km to the north of Neapoli. Minoan Milatos stood between the modern village and the fine sandy beach which is 1 km. away. In the myths, Milatos was a boy who, like Romulus and Remus, was brought up in the forest by a she-wolf. When he grew up, he killed the tyrant of the city and escaped to Asia Minor, where he was said to have founded the famous city of Miletus (Milatos being a Doric form of Miletus), where the revolt of the Greek cities against the Persians began in 499 BC. In the 3rd century BC Milatos was destroyed by Lyttos.

Near the village, in a deep gorge, is the historic **Milatos cave**. It has eight entrances spaced out over 40 metres of the cliff-face and on three different levels, and it has a total area of 2,100 square metres. There are no particularly interesting geological phenomena in the cave, but it is famous for its historical connections. Here, in 1823, a large number of women and children took shelter from the Turks, who surrounded the cave and cut off the escape of its occupants. When the Greeks were forced to surrender, 15 days later, Husein Bey, who was in charge of the Turkish forces, slaughtered all the old men and the few fighting troops and sold the women and children into slavery in Egypt.

After visiting the pretty town of **Neapoli**, we begin to climb towards the Laisithi plateau, which lies high in the Mt Dikti range, at a height of 817-850 metres. The plateau, which occupies an area of 2,500 hectares, is surrounded by the high peaks of the range. Thanks to the geological composition of the ground, the plateau retains the rainfall and some 10,000 windmills raise the water from wells to irrigate the plain; apart from being picturesque, they also make the plain among the most fertile parts of Crete.

Archaeological investigation has shown that the Lasithi Plateau was occupied as early as Neolithic times (Trapeza Cave, Diktaean Cave). Settlements have been found at Karfi and Plati. In historical times, the area was part of the territory of the city-state of Lyttos. Under Byzantium, there was a large town at Avgoustis. In 1263, however, the Venetians drove out all the inhabitants of the plateau, which had become a centre of resistance to their rule. They forbade any cultivation of the fields, on pain of death. And so for two whole centuries the plain lay fallow, its villages deserted and its fields waterlogged in winter. But when the Venetians had to deal with a shortage of wheat, they were compelled to allow the plateau to be farmed and inhabited again. They also helped to drain the area, digging the ditches which can still be seen today.

Today, the plateau is in the Eparchy of Lasithi; it has a total of 21 villages organised into 12 communes (administrative units). Thanks to its healthy climate, the fame of the Diktaean Cave and the spontaneous and unselfish hospitality of its people, it has become a major tourist attraction.

We leave Neapoli and take the left fork, heading south. The road passes through the pretty village of **Vryses** and enters the verdant valley of Drasi. Now we begin to climb, with bend after bend, and we pass the villages of **Apano** and **Kato Amygdali** and **Zenia**. At 29 km. from Ayios Nikolaos and at an altitude of 850 m., we pass the village of **Exo Potami**. A further three kilometres through a green valley where the vegetation is dominated by ilexes brings us to **Mesa Potami**, a picturesque village standing at 880 metres above sea level. The road continues to wind upwards, and at the spot known as 'tou Patera ta Sellia', reaches its highest point, at an altitude of 1100 metres. The view all around is superb, with the wild beauty of the gorge behind us and the plateau, with its white windmills breaking the otherwise static landscape, stretching out in front.

The road now runs downhill into the plateau. At 39 km. we come to the first village on the plateau, **Mesa Lasithi**, which stands at an altitude of 870 m. From here a side-road to the right leads to the **Kroustallenias Monastery**. This foundation, with its wonderful view, stands nestling against a rock covered with ancient maples and oaks and clad in ivy which winds itself round the trunks and branches of the trees.

The monastery was founded around 1540 and is dedicated to the Dormition of the Virgin. It takes its name, which means 'of crystal', from an icon of Our Lady which was found here, painted on crystal. The monastery played an important part in the struggle for Greek liberation, which is why the Turks destroyed it twice, and in the field of learning: it housed what was until 1870 the only primary school in Lasithi.

The fertile plateau with its 10,000 white windmills.

44 km. Tzermiado, the principal town of the Eparchy of Lasithi. This village, on the southern slopes of Mt Selena, has the excellent climate of all the plateau and was first founded in the 15th century. Archaeological finds from the Middle Minoan period have come to light in the area.

To the east of Tzermiado is the **Trapeza cave**, which is thought to be the earliest centre of cult worship on the plateau and is of great archaeological interest. It was first used as a dwelling-place, and later, when the habitations moved to the Kastelos hill to the east of Tzermiado, it became a burial-place and shrine. Systematic ar-chaeological investigation has brought to light finds from all the periods between the Neolithic and the Byzantine, which means that it continued to be used even after its position as a centre of worship had been usurped by the Diktaean Cave.

43 km. Ayios Yeorgios. Here we should stop to visit the **Folklore Museum of Crete**. In a lovely house dating from 1800, a strict example of the local style of architecture, and in an adjacent more modern building restored to the style of a middle-class residence of the early 20th century, are the Museum's collections. These are arranged in harmonious order and in a functional form so as to provide a picture of traditional life in the home and in the fields; there are complete sets of equipment for iron-working, cheese-making, basket-weaving, a host of domestic utensils, a traditional fireplace, looms, an oven, a plough, a boiler for distilling raki, and much, much more. One room is devoted to the folk painters and wood-carvers of Crete. Also on show are delicately-woven textiles in traditional patterns, finely-worked wooden furniture, hanging lamps, a wealth of photographs and other documentary evidence and even weapons.

The road continues through the attractive villages of

In the half-dark the stalactites glimmer: the forms of Zeus, of Hera, of Artemis and of Athena can be seen. At the back of the cave, above the pure water of a little lake, a forest of stalactites known as "the cloak of Zeus" is reflected in the water like a gigantic candelabrum.

Avrakontes and **Kaminaki** and at 47 km. enters **Psychro** (at an altitude of 840 m.), also first built in the 15th century. The village owes its name (which means 'cold') to a spring called Psychro from which it takes its water or, according to other sources, to the fact that the weather is often cold.

The road ends at the NTOG pavilion. From here it is a 15-minute walk (donkeys are also available) to the magnificent entry to the Diktaean Cave.

The **Diktaean Cave** stands at an altitude of 1025 metres on the northern slopes of Mt Dikti. This, according to the myths, was the place where Zeus, the father of gods and men, was born. Wonder and

awe overcome one at the sight of the enormous entrance to the cave, crowned by trees and bushes and surrounding by wild flowers whose aroma fills the air. As one begins the descent into the cave, the atmosphere changes and becomes more solemn and suggestive, redolent of religious significance. The light of one's candle or torch is one's only companion. Huge stalactities hang from the ceiling, like giants whose backs have for countless centuries been supporting the roof of the cave. The damp atmosphere and the deathly silence are broken only by the fluttering of the occasional wild dove; birds still nest in the cave.

In was here, in this magnificent cave, that Rhea took refuge and, with the help of her mother Gea, gave birth to Zeus, the divine infant. The cave extended its generous protection to the baby and managed to save it from the murderous plans of its father Kronos, who, fearing that one of his offspring would take his throne from him, devoured them all as soon as Rhea gave birth to them. It could be said that the Diktaean Cave stands to pagan religion as Bethlehem stands to Christianity.

The Diktaean Cave consists of two parts. The first or northerly part, the antechamber, is flat and has a total length of 42 m., a width of 19 m. and a height of

Life in Lasithi.

3. Kritsa, Lato Hetera

We leave Ayios Nikolaos in a southerly direction, taking the Siteia road. At 1.5 km. we turn right, following a good surfaced road. We pass on our right a turning for the Lasithi Plateau.

The road crosses a verdant plain with olive and almond trees; at 7 km it passes the little village of **Mardati**. At little before it reaches the village, at the spot known as 'Logari', 100 metres to the right of the road, we can see the gleaming white church of **Kera Panayia**. This is a three-aisled building, dedicated to the Dormition of the Virgin, St Anne and St Anthony. It is rectangular and domed and was built in three stages, between the 13th and mid-14th centuries. The interior is decorated with fine murals: the *Pantocrator*, near the entrance, four *Angels*, many saints, the *Birth of Christ, St Anne,* the *Virgin*, the *Ascension, Paradise* and the *Punishment of the Damned* -an artistic treasure of the 14th and 15th century, a period when the Venetians ruled Crete, but allowed the islanders to build and decorate their churches as they wished.

At 11 km the road enters the large village of **Kritsa**. This is an attractive place, built in ampitheatre style on the foothills of the Kastellos mountain, with wonderful views of the plain of olives and almonds which stretches out below it and the tranquil gulf of Mirabello. This is a village which has retained its traditional Cretan colour, both in its whitewashed two-storey houses, with the elaborate ironwork of their balconies and the picturesque alleyways, and in the age-old occupations of the residents

6.5 m. Here an altar had been built and around it were tables for offerings, statuettes in stances of devotion, Kamares ware pottery and other items. The second part, which runs from north to south, is the main cave and slopes downward. Its total length is 85 m., its width is 38 m. and its height is between 5 and 14 m. At the back on the left is a further small chamber, and tradition has it that a hidden recess in it is where Zeus was born. On the right is the lake, whose dimensions are 16 × 8.5 metres.

It was only natural that this enormous cave, with its wealth of stalactites, its dark and menacing atmosphere and also its ease of access to man should

develop into a shrine. And it was also natural that together with the deities worshipped here the stalactites should also become the objects of devotion, as can be seen from the votive offerings found among their folds. The finds which archaeologists have discovered the Diktaean Cave are more ancient than those in the Idaean Cave, which justifies the point of view that Zeus was born in the Diktaean Cave but brought up in the Idaean Cave, where he was taken by the Kouretes.

49 km. Plati. This village, built in a fertile landscape where fruit trees flourish on the lower slopes of Mt Afentis Christos, is of considerable archaeological interest.

—particularly those of the women, who work at the loom— as well as the strict observance of the local customs. Its textiles, embroidery and knitting are renowned for their design and colours.

There has been a village here since Roman times. It was destroyed by the Arabs, but rebuilt in the 10th century. Under the Venetians it was the biggest village in Crete, and continued to be so until recently. Because of its involvement in all the uprisings of the Cretans, it was repeatedly damaged in reprisals. Kritsa has a number of decorated Byzantine churches. Of these, after Our Lady Kera, the three-aisled church of St John the Divine, built in the Late Byzantine period and constituting a dependency of the Toplou Monastery, is the most important.

Kritsa was chosen by the French director Jules Dassen for the filming of his masterpiece *Celui qui faut mourir*, based on the novel by Kazantzakis *Greek Passion*, an ideal book for the visitor who is in Crete for Easter, the year's most important festival in Greece, to have with him. It was here also that another of Kazantzakis' novels —*Christ Re-crucified*— was filmed.

An earth track leaves Kritsa in a northerly direction and after approximately 3 km reaches the ruins of the ancient city of **Lato**.

These imposing archaic remains form an amphitheatre in a valley between two mountain peaks. The landscape is isolated, idyllic and covered with flowers in the spring. Great simplicity and peace reign here, while the view, from the sea to the mountains of Lasithi, is captivating.

The city was built in the 7th century BC by the Dorians and

Our Lady 'Kera'.

took its name from Leto, the mother of Apollo and Artemis ('Lato' being the Doric form of 'Leto'). It was called 'Hetera' (= 'other') Lato to distinguish it from the Lato towards Kamara which is the present-day Ayios Nikolaos, which was its port.

The archaeological site is entered from the west, through the gate of the city from which a stepped road leads uphill. At the top of the road uphill, between two hills, is the agora, which is pentagonal and served not only as a centre for trade, but also for politics and culture. The remains of an arcade, a temple, a water tank and a banqueting

hall with benches and a staircase are to be found here. The steps are similar to those in Minoan theatres. The Prytaneum (administative headquarters) is behind this theatre area. The walls and buildings which we can see today belong chiefly to the 5th and 4th centuries BC.

4. Mochlos, Siteia

We leave Ayios Nikolaos along the coast road for Siteia as far as Pacheia Ammos. We pass the turning for Ierapetra and at 27 km. we reach the village of **Kavousi**, which stands in a fertile valley full of olive trees and crossed by a seasonal river. Kavousi Bay is at the end of the Gulf of Mirabello, on the edge of one of the largest plantations of olive trees on Crete. There is a spring with cool water and plane trees, an ideal spot for a drink and to look at the view. In the village, there is a little medieval church of St George, above the central square. It was built in the time of the Venetian occupation but in the Byzantine style.

Ancient Cambousi, which stood on the slopes of the hill above the modern village, was the first archaeological site in Crete to be investigated by American scholars.

From Kavousi it is possible to ascend the steep sides of Mt Kapsas. The Gulf of Mirabello ends here.

The road begins to climb, crossing the picturesque valley of Lastros, where the village of the same name lies between two hilltops, and at 40 km. comes to the village of **Sfaka**. From here, a track runs down to the seaside and leads to the attractive fishing-village of **Mochlos**. Although the area is in the process of rapid tourist development, Mochlos is still an ideal place for quiet and relaxation. From its attractive cafés there is a unique view along the steep rocky coastline.

From Mochlos there are boat trips to the islets of Ayios Nikolaos and Pseira.

Ayios Nikolaos lies directly off Mochlos. There is a chapel to St Nicholas on it. In antiquity, the island formed a peninsula jutting out from the mainland, with bays on its eastern and western sides. In the Early Minoan period there was a prosperous settlement in the area, since this was the first port at which ships sailing to Crete from the Middle East and Egypt called. Interesting tombs, which are rather reminiscent of houses, have been found on the western slopes of the rock. The 'treasure of Mochlos', which is today in Herakleio Museum, consists largely of gold jewellery; it includes a superb diadem decorated with animal motifs. Also in the treasure were bronze tools and weapons which must have been made from bronze imported from Cyprus, Minoan double axes, and fine stone

Mochlos, with the islet of Ayios Nikolaos.

Siteia stands on the slopes of a low hill.

vases in decorating which the skilled artisans had made use of the natural grain of the stone. From these finds it would appear that the islet was a centre for prehistoric shipping.

To the west of Mochlos is the barren little island of **Pseira**, which is uninhabited today. In Minoan times, it had an important settlement by the natural harbour on the east side of the island, which is suitable for small vessels. The Romans built a camp on the island's highest point.

We return to Sfaka. The road continues to climb, and at 42 km. comes to the village of **Tourloti**, which stands on top of a hill called Kastri. There are remains of an ancient city in the vicinity, and statuettes and pottery have

been found.

After Tourloti we come, on our left, to **Myrsini**, where shaft graves have been excavated.

At 51 km. is the village of **Mesa Mouliana**, which stands on an amphitheatrical site in an area heavily planted with vines. The famous Mouliana wine is made here. In the village itself, two tholos tombs have been found; they were used during the Early Geometric period, at which time the dead were cremated, and during Mycenean times, when they were entombed. A vase decorated with a representation of a mounted warrior —the only one of its kind discovered in Crete— was also found here.

We continue, passing at 53 km. through the village of **Exo Mouliana**, which has a church

of St George with wall-paintings. At 59 km. we come to **Hamezi**, an attractive upland village. To the south of the village is the famous 'Oval House', a fortress-like building of the Middle Minoan period. The village Folklore Museum is worth a visit; it has interesting collections of all kinds of folklore items. Among the exhibits is a unique loom with all its weaving equipment. In late September every year, the village is the scene of the 'Kazanemata', the festival to mark the traditional distilling of tsikoudia, the national drink of Crete, which is followed by general jollification.

After Hamezi the road begins to run downhill, passing through the village of **Skopi** before arriving in the attractive town of Siteia.

Siteia, which is the capital of the Eparchy by the same name, stands at the head of Siteia Bay, which is the most easterly of the large inlets on the north side of the island. Its amphitheatrical site occupies the sides of a low hill. This pleasant coastal town continues today to have much of the calm and charm of bygone days. The landscape here is not so wild as elsewhere on Crete, and the mountain ranges on the horizon are much gentler: none of them exceeds 800 metres in height. The surrounding countryside is green and fertile. The beach, with its fine, white sand, running down to clear blue waters, is a constant invitation to bathe. The local residents, too, are lovers of peace and quiet; cheerful and hospitable, they are known for their pleasure in music and feasting.

The modern city stands on the site of ancient **Eteia**, which was the port of Praisos. This is the area where the Eteocretans

Siteia, a hospitable coastal town.

lived: they were the indigenous islanders who retreated to isolated areas when the Dorian invasion occurred so as to avoid intermingling with the interlopers. The port gained in strength after 146 BC, when the people of Praisos settled there on the destruction of their own city by Ierapetra. Eteia continued to flourish throughout the Roman, Byzantine (when it was the seat of a bishopric, later moved to the village of Episkopi) and Venetian periods.

In 1508, the town was destoyed by an earthquake and in 1538 it was sacked by pirates. After this it went into decline, and in 1651 it was abandoned by its inhabitants, who moved to the district of Liopetro. At about this time, the Venetians themselves ruined their own castle to prevent it falling into the hands of the Turks. These ruins can still be seen today, to the east of the town. Only a tower with three floors has survived, together with some other buildings protected by a polygonal defensive wall with battlements. This section of wall crowned the eastern wing of the castle. Before the Venetians, the Genoese had build a fortress in Siteia in 1204, on the foundations of earlier Byzantine buildings. Some remains of Roman fishing installations can be seen near the Customs House. On the northern side of the fortress, there was under the Venetians the **Santa Maria Monastery**, which was demolished by the Turks. On its ruins was built a little chapel, and since then the area has been used as a cemetery. The town itself was rebuilt in 1870 to plans by the progressive Turk Avni Pasha.

Siteia was the birthplace of the famous Cretan poet Vincenzo Kornaros, who wrote his verse-play *Erotokritos* to narrate the adventures of Princess Arethusa and Prince Erotokritos. *Erotokritos* is the outstanding masterpiece of the Cretan literary school and despite the three centuries which have passed since it was written, it continues to be sung and performed today.

Examples of the prosperity and culture of the ancient city can be admired in the **Archaeological Museum**, which has been housed in a modern building since 1984 and is the third-largest in Crete. On display are finds from the wider area around Siteia and from the palace at Zakro; they are arranged in such a way as to provide visitors with a most informative tour. The town also has a **Folklore Museum**, with collections of textiles, embroidery, local costumes, traditional furniture and domestic utensils which give visitors a full picture of what life used to be like in these parts. At the theatre, which is against the renovated part of the city wall, there are interesting cultural events each summer.

There are ferry sailings from Siteia to the Dodecanese, the Aegean Islands and Kavala in northern Greece. Since 1984 there has also been an airport, which is only 10 minutes from the centre of town.

The pretty little harbour of Siteia, from where the ships sail to the Dodecannese.

Siteia will be our starting point for visits to the archaeological sites of Palaikastro, Zakro and Praisos. We shall also be making the acquaintance of the historic Toplou Monastery and going to Vai for a swim in wonderful natural surroundings.

5. Toplou Monasteri, Vai

We leave Siteia and head east. At 5 km. from the town we come to **Ayia Fotia**, a pretty little seaside village with a fine beach. The houses date from Venetian times and have recently been renovated. Near the village, Greek archaeologists have discovered the largest Early Minoan cemetery ever found, with 250 tombs of all sizes. Among the finds which they discovered are vases and clay and stone objects which can be seen today in the museums of Ayios Nikolaos and Siteia.

Our road continues, and at 12 km. from Siteia comes to a crossroads. We take the turning to the left and after 8 km. come to the historic **Toplou Monastery**.

The monastery rises fortress-like out of an arid landscape. It is also known as Our Lady 'of the Cape' ('Akrotiriani') because of its proximity to Cape Sidero. It acquired the name of Toplou in Turkish times because it had a cannon ('top') since Venetian days to protect itself from pirates. In its current form, it dates from the 17th century, but the wall-paintings in the church make it plain that the original buildings go back to the 14th century.

The Monastery is square, with the ground-plan of a fortress and a total area of 800 square metres. There are three

"Great Art Thou, O Lord": a portable icon in Toplou Monastery, 1770.

storeys, and the whole structure is surrounded by a wall. Among the principal features is the belfry, which stands to a height of 33 metres; it has crowns in relief and bears the date 1558. In the little inner courtyard is a well which never runs dry and which supplies the monastery's water. Opposite the well is the twin-aisled basilica which is the main monastery church, dedicated to the Nativity of Our Lady and to St John the Divine. To the left, before we enter the church, is an important 2nd century BC inscrip-

tion referring to an alliance between the cities of Itanos and Ierapytna.

Among the important portable icons in the church is one by Ioannis Kornaros known as 'Great Art Thou, O Lord', dating from 1770. The paintings in the north aisle are from the 14th century. The icon of Our Lady was found in a cave where there is a spring; its water is regarded as holy.

In 1662, the monastery collapsed during an earthquake but was soon rebuilt. In 1821 it suffered further severe damage. It has been stavro-

pegic (under the protection of the Patriarchate of Constantinople) since 1704, and this helped it to survive despite the inevitable depredations of the Turks. Before Crete was free, it was a centre for revolutionary meeting and provided shelter for freedom fighters on the run from the authorities. A secret school operated there throughout the period of Turkish rule. During the German occupation, the Toplou Monastery had a secret wireless post. It was also one of the richest monasteries on Crete, and even today large tracts of land round about belong to it. At the height of its prosperity, it had 150 monks. Its feast day is on 26 Septemper, when there is a great festival which attracts large numbers of pilgrims.

From the Toplou Monastery, the good, surfaced road continues north east for Vai. At 25 km. there is a turning (right) for Palaikastro. We continue north, and after a further 2 km. a road to the right takes us down to the beach through the famous palm forest of **Vai**.

The 5,000 palm trees stand in an attractive valley between two hills, arranged amphitheatrically and overlooking the golden beach. Here the landscape has changed once more: now it is tropical and idyllic.

According to the myths, the existence of the palm trees was attributed to the Phoenicians, who called here and threw away the stones of the dates they were eating. The trees, 'vayia' in the local dialect, have given Vai its name. Today the whole area and all routes of access to the beach are carefully fenced off and camping is strictly forbidden. The main entrance is open from sunrise to sunset, and so the calm and beauty of the landscape can still be enjoyed while sipping a cool drink in one of the pretty little cafés.

We return to the side-road for the beach and turn right (north) for Itanos.

After about 3 km. the road ends at a quiet sandy bay, **Erimoupoli**. This is the site of one of the most important cities of eastern Crete, ancient **Itanos**. The name comes from Itanos, one of the Kouretes who brought up Zeus. According to the myths, the Argonauts built a temple to Athena here. As archaeological finds have shown, Itanos was occupied between Minoan times and the Christian era. There was a large harbour, which would have acted as a way-station on the routes between Crete and the Middle East. The city was autonomous, and had a number of other settlements under its control. Later, however, Dragmos —one of these subject cities— overcame it.

When the Romans came to Crete, Itanos began to flourish once again, minting its own coins, most of which depict Tritons, reasonably enough in view of its sea-faring traditions. The city continued to prosper in the early Byzantine period, when marvellous churches were built. But in the 9th century it was destroyed by the Saracens, or, according to other sources, its decline was due to an earthquake in 795 which caused the ground to subside. In the 15th century it was razed by pirates. Among the finds from the site, there is particular interest in a 2nd century BC inscription which refers to a dispute between Itanos and Ierapythna over a shrine to Zeus Diktaios. Another find of importance is the inscription which today can be seen at Toplou Monastery. Epitaphs from the Early Christian period have come to light, and there are remains of a large Byzantine basilica.

6. Palaikastro, Kato Zakros

We head back the way we came, passing the turning for the beach, and at 25 km. take the road left for **Palaikastro**. This village lies in the most easterly part of the Prefecture. 2 km away is its beach, with a fine expanse of sand and a natural harbour looking out to the islet of Grandes. Near the village important Minoan remains have come to light. At the spot known as Rousolakkos, the spades of the archaeologists have uncovered a Middle Minoan settlement. The main road running through the centre of the town was intersected by smaller streets at right angles to it, separating off the different neighbourhoods with their impressive house facades.

In the same area is the wonderful **Shrine of Zeus Diktaios**. Among the ruins and the other important finds was an inscription recording the hymn to Cretan Zeus which youths sang in the temple, while dancing the dance of the Kouretes.

To the south of Palaikastro is the steep hill of **Petsofas**. On the summit, an open-air shrine of the Middle Minoan period has been excavated and has produced important finds, including a number of fine statuettes, 10-17 cm. in height, representing people in attitudes of prayer.

From Palaikastro we take the difficult uphill road to Zakro. At 38 km we reach the attractive village of **Epano Zakros**, which stands on two hills covered with fruit trees and olives. Cobbled lanes lead between the whitewashed houses with their charming courtyards. From the village square a surfaced road leads to an attractive sheltered bay where the village of **Kato Zakros** stands. Here recent investigation has revealed a large

Minoan palace, the fourth largest in Crete and the only one to have escaped robbery. It was built around 1600 BC, covered an area of 8,000 square metres and had 180 rooms.

Most of the excavations on the site were the work of professor Platon. Although smaller than Knossos or Phaistos, it was laid out along the same lines. There was a central paved court with three entrances to the west and an altar in front of the main entrance. On the western side were the official apartments. On the north side were light shafts, kitchens, a dining-room and large basins which must have been used in cult worship. In the Treasury a number of superb vases were found. The eastern side contained the principal living apartments, while the south side of the court consisted mostly of workshops. Among the most interesting finds from the site are vases decorated with olives which look as if they have just been harvested, long swords encrusted with sheets of gold, bronze decorative objects from Cyprus.

The site of the palace is of great importance, since standing as it does on the east coast of Crete it would be in an ideal position to import goods from the East and sell them to the other palaces. Thus its harbour developed into a major commercial port and the whole Minoan 'thalassocracy' relied heavily upon it.

Ruins of a Minoan villa have come to light near the 'Gorge of the Dead' ('Farangi ton Nekron'), so-called because this was the cemetery for all the various settlements, as proved by the tombs which have been excavated.

Apart from the value of its archaeological site, Kato Zakros is also a wonderful place, with a fine sandy beach and clear blue waters: an invitation for a swim.

The archaeological site at Kato Zakro.

7. Episkopi, Praisos

We now leave Siteia along the road which passes in front of the Museum, heading south for Lithines. After about 2.5 km. we come to the village of **Maranes**, where a Minoan villa of the Late Palace period has been discovered. A little further along, a side road some 5 km. in length leads to another Minoan villa near the village of **Zou**, from whose springs the water supply of Siteia is run.

The road continues and after 4 km. comes to the pretty village of **Piskokefalo**, which stands near the old village of Kato Episkopi on the hill of Kefalo from which it takes its name. Under the Venetians, this area belonged to the feudal estate of the Kornaros family. There is a fine old church of St George, dating from the 15th century. Professor Platon the archaeologist concluded from the archaeological finds on the site, and particularly from the statuettes of men and women in attitudes of prayer, that

there must have been a shrine here rather like that of Petsofas. However, the statuettes yielded by this site are of a more sophisticated technique; the female figurines have cunning hair-styles, hats and rich clothing. They are of exceptional importance for the study of ancient clothing and hairdressing in Crete.

Piskokefalo is another village where the 'Kazanemata', the traditional late-September feast to celebrate the making of the 'tsikoudia' is held. There are large-scale festivities with much consumption of the local delicacies.

The road continues, passing at 9 km. the village of **Maronia** and at 12 km. that of **Epano Episkopi**, which in the 16th century was the seat of the Bishop of Siteia. Here the road forks. To the right (south west), the road leads to Lithines and then on to Ierapetra. We take the left-hand turning, which heads south east and after crossing a fertile valley comes to **Nea Praisos** at 17 km. Arrows point

the way to the site of ancient **Praisos**, which was an Eteocretan town. The oldest settlement was near the ruins we see today, and in the 12th century BC the Eteocretans and Dorians built a new city, spread over three hills and surrounded by walls, remains of which can be seen today. The city was autonomous, with its own coinage and domination over a wide area. To the north, it had a port on the Cretan Sea at Siteia and to the south another at Steles, on the Libyan Sea, as demonstrated by an inscription which has come to light in archaeological investigations. In 145 BC the city was destroyed by Ierapytna.

Overall, however, this site was occupied from the Stone Age to Venetian times. Excavations have revealed Hellenistic houses, the foundations of a temple, tholos tombs and various other objects.

We continue, passing the village of **Handras** at 26 km. from Siteia and **Ziros** at 31 km. Here there is a church of St Paraskevi, with wall-paintings.

Ierapetra, a modern town on an indented coastline with golden beaches.

8. Pacheia Ammos, Ierapetra

We leave the town of Ayios Nikolaos along the pretty coast road for Ierapetra and Siteia, heading initially south. At 4-6 km. from the town we pass an attractive resort area where the hotels and the other buildings are in the harmonious style of the Aegean islands.

Shortly before we reach Gournia there is a crossroads from which a passable unsurfaced road leads in approximately 8 km. to the **Faneromeni Monastery**. This foundation stands in an isolated site high up in the mountains, amid fine scenery. Its twin-aisled little church stands inside a cave, where an icon of Our Lady was revealed ('fanerothike', hence the name) to the faithful. On 15-16 August there is a major religious and secular feast here, which attracts many people from the surrounding areas. At

19 km. along the main road, on the right, there is a large Minoan settlement at the spot known as **Gournia**. The ancient name of this site remains unknown to us, while the modern name is derived from the small ancient cisterns ('gournes') discovered here before the main excavations took place. According to the archaeologists, the settlement was built around 1600 BC, on a low, flat-topped hill, and it occupied an area of more than 15,000 square metres. Around 1450 BC —that is, only 150 years later— it was destroyed in the same catastrophe which struck the other large Minoan palaces. It was never rebuilt.

This site has been described by the archaeologists as the remains of a primarily commercial city; many tools came to light here (saws, lathes, needles, hooks, etc.). It was not rich, and the king lived close to his subjects, as can be seen from the houses clustered around his

palace. However, the site is of great archaeological value for the light it sheds on the ordinary everyday life of the Minoans and their daily occupations.

We continue along the main road, and at 21 km. come to **Pacheia Ammos**. As the name suggests (it means 'thick sand'), there is a fine sandy beach here. The surrounding area is also attractive, with dense olive groves and hothouses. One kilometre further along we come to a crossroads, where we leave behind the road to Siteia and head south for Ierapetra. This part of the island, from Pacheia Ammos to Ierapetra, is the narrowest area of Crete, being only 12 km. broad. After about 3 km. a side-road to the right leads to the village of **Vasiliki**, whose archaeological sites were explored by Richard Seager. Its importance lies in the fact that some of the island's few surviving Early Palace period buildings (2600-2000 BC) were found here. The sophisticated houses (and in particular the 'House on the Hill') were the forerunners of the magnificent palaces built later on. The 'House on the Hill' was a little palace in its own right, with a paved court on the western side and impressively large rectangular rooms where traces of red plaster can still be seen on the walls.

At 29 km. we pass the pretty village of **Kato Chorio** with its abundant streams and thick vegetation, and we soon come to **Ierapetra**, the most southerly town in all Greece.

The site of the modern town was occupied by one of the most important cities in ancient Crete. It was initially called Cyrbas, from the name of its founder; according to the myths, Cyrbas was one of the artisans whom Rhea brought with her from Rhodes. Later it was called Kamiros,, Pytna, Ierapetra and eventually Ierapetra. It reached the height of its prosperity in the 2nd century BC, when it dominated Praisos and almost the whole of the Siteia area. As an independent and autonomous city, it minted its own coins, which showed tripods and wreaths or the head of Zeus and a palm-tree. It resisted the Romans bravely, and was the last Cretan city to be conquered and destroyed by them, in 66 BC. However, it was soon rebuilt and regained its former eminence. Up to the 10th century there were two theatres, numerous places of worship, an amphitheatre, an aqueduct and statuary which demonstrated its prosperity. In 824 it was laid waste by the Saracens, and in 1508 it was flattened by an earthquake. In Venetian times, Morosini built a fortress here on the site of an earlier castle; his rectangular building had towers at all four corners, an inner courtyard and a water tank. Remains of this building can still be seen today (called the 'Koules'). In 1647 the town was taken by the Turks, who renovated the fortress and added new buildings to it. Remnants of the presence of the Turks can still be seen today in the old town, with its pretty alleys and low houses. There is also a mosque with an inscription over its door; opposite stands a reconstructed Turkish fountain. In Dimarcheiou Square is the Ottoman School or Mehtep, which today is used for various cultural activities.

In 1798, it is said that Napoleon spent the night in the town on the way to Egypt, and the house in which he stayed can still be seen.

The sea front, the harbour and the old castle in the background.

Nearby beaches can be reached by caique from Ierapetra.

East from Ierapetra

We leave Ierapetra and head east, taking the surfaced coast road. After almost 16 km we reach **Ayia Fotia** ∣ This village, concealed by tall pines, stands in an idyllic spot and has a fine sandy beach.

We continue through the coastal villages of **Galini, Achlia, Mavro Kalymno, Ayios Pantaleimon** and **Koutsouras**. At 24 km. from Ierapetra we come to the pretty seaside village of **Makriyialos**, on the attractive bay of Kala Nera. This village has developed into an important tourist resort thanks to its long beach, with white sand and clear blue waters. Next to the modern village church, archaeological investigations have revealed a Minoan villa. A villa dating from Roman times in the same area has also been explored.

The road continues along the coast to the pretty village of **Analipsi**, after which it turns left and heads north for Siteia.

From Analipsi, a passable unsurfaced road along the coast leads in about 9 km. to the **Kapsa Monastery**, which stands near the shore, on a steep-sided rock close to the fine Perivolakia Gorge. The monastery is believed to have been founded in the 15th century, though in 1471 it was laid waste by pirates and abandoned. In 1841 it was renovated by Yerontoyannis, a reformed robber who lived there as a hermit. He built the church, dedicated to John the Baptist, and added new cells. Today the monastery is run by Toplou Monastery.

Its feast day is on 29 August, when there is a large secular festival.

The little **Archaeological Museum** of Ierapetra contains exhibits dating from between Early Minoan and Roman times, including inscriptions and statues, mostly from Vasiliki and Gournia. The most interesting exhibits are the fine though rather crude larnaces from Episkopi, fashioned from clay and decorated with pictures of animals in lively colours. There is also a fine Roman statue discovered in Ierapetra; it stands 1.5 metres high and shows the goddess Demeter (Ceres) holding a bunch of wheat. There are two little snakes entwined in her hair.

The town also has a number of interesting churches dating from more modern times, with carved wooden screens and important icons.

Today, Ierapetra is an attractive modern town; the indented coastline has some superb sandy beaches. Thanks to its mild climate and generally good weather, it has the most sunshine and the least rainfall of anywhere else in Crete, making it an ideal spot for holidays summer and winter. It is also one of the most important fruit and vegetable-growing centres in Greece, since the climatic conditions are favourable to early crops. Something of an industrial centre, it is particularly noted for the manufacture of knives.

From Ierapetra there are beaches to visit both east and west of the town and on the islet of Chrysi.

Chrysi lies about 15 km. off the coast to the south of Ierapetra. As the name indicates (it means 'the golden one'), the islet's beaches have fine golden sand running down into greenish-blue water. The harmony of the landscape is supplemented by a forest of cader trees. Throughout the summer, boats and launches run to the islet from Ierapetra, sailing out in the morning and returning in the late afternoon.

Makriyalos.

Mirtos: the Minoan villa at Pyrgos.

West from Ierapetra

At approximately 5 km. we come to the seaside village of **Gra-Lygia**. The village runs down to a long beach with coarse sand.

The road continues in the direction of Myrtos. At about 10 km. from Ierapetra, on a hill to the right of the road at the spot known as 'Fournou i Koryfi', a Minoan settlement has been discovered. Shortly before we enter Myrtos, a path to the right of the road leads to a low hill, on which, at the spot known as 'Pyrgos', a second Minoan settlement has come to light. On the top of this hill, the spades of the archaeologists revealed a large villa which must have stood 2 or 3 storeys in height. It belonged to the Late Palace period.

Myrtos, 16 km. from Ierapetra, is an attractive village, which stands on the banks of the Kryos river and has an attractive beach with fine sand and clear waters. From Myrtos the road continues to the north west for Vianos and Herakleio.

A complete guide for drivers and travellers · scale 1:200.000